THE WILD GOURMET

The Wild Gourmet

A FORAGER'S COOKBOOK

by *BABETTE BRACKETT*

and *MARYANN LASH*

DAVID R. GODINE, PUBLISHER

BOSTON

David R. Godine, Publisher
306 Dartmouth Street
Boston, Massachusetts 02116
Copyright©1975 by David R. Godine
Manufactured in the United States of America
ISBN 0-87923-132-7, hardcover.
        0-87923-142-4, softcover.
LCC 75-25953.

Designed by Philip Grushkin
Cover photograph by James McGaw

Contents

JULY

AUGUST

SEPTEMBER

OCTOBER

NOVEMBER

Acknowledgments

We are truly grateful to our many friends who have shared their cooking lore with us. Some are rooted in New England. Others draw their cooking styles from the four corners of the globe. To all of them we wish to say thank you. Friends, relatives and neighbors who have lent a hand include Anni Amberger, Peg Anderson, Missy Arsenian, Toby Arsenian, Margaret Bassett, Ray Bentley, Barbara Brackett, Katharine Brackett, Marilyn Cahill, Helvi Carter, David Cohen, M.D., Sarah Dunlap, Rand Engel, Amelia Fisk, Kitty Fitts, Constance Gibson, Priscilla Jamison, Lucy Kimball, Nan Paget, Winifred Perkins, Robert Sampson, Patricia and David Sharpe, Navin Shah, Elizabeth G. Smith, Roger T. Twitchell, Steve Warshall, Barbara Wolfe, and Noel and Frances Yauch. Finally, we must mention our husbands and children, without whom this book would have been impossible: Joshua and Mallory and Anna, Cynthia, Nathan and Stephanie.

Pigeon Cove, Massachusetts   *BABETTE BRACKETT*

September 1974   *MARYANN LASH*

SIMPLE GIFTS

'Tis the gift to be simple, 'tis the gift to be free.
'Tis the gift to come down where we ought to be.
And when we find ourselves in the place just right
'Twill be in the valley of love and delight.
When true simplicity is gain'd,
To bow and to bend, we shan't be ashamed.
To turn, turn, will be our delight
'Till by turning, turning we come round right.

Shaker song, c. 1845

Introduction

I

*J*ust as the seasons turn and turn, the things that grow on the earth follow in their turn. It's no use trying to find fresh day lily blossoms in October, mushrooms in February or blueberries in April.

We have attempted in *The Wild Gourmet* to start you on the way to knowing the rhythms of growth, flowering and fruiting (and some rooting) in the Northeast. Many edibles we include are also found in other parts of the United States and, of course, the world. A calendar, with its numbers, is one part of our lives. Another part, which we hope will come hand-in-hand to you, is nature's changing face through the year. A simple way to link these two truths is by eating according to the seasons—eating the things that are growing on their own, in fields, woods, meadows, your back yard, on rocks beside the ocean, cracks in the sidewalk and wherever else seeds, runners, roots and bulbs can survive.

We have avoided complicated directions for canning and freezing which would take you away from the natural cycle of change and put you back on the numbers and dates level. We feel attuned to Thoreau when he said, "I love best to have each thing in its season only, and enjoy doing without it all other times."

The season for each wilding given here is only approximate. Weather and local variations of heat, moisture and fertility will affect the growing pattern. Don't worry if you are a week "late." There probably is considerable latitude in your particular latitude.

Don't be disappointed if you can't find a plant just where it is supposed to be. Nature's supermarket is a little on the casual side. But it is also full of nice surprises. You may find, as we did one day, a beautiful batch of cranberries while on a mushroom expedition. Foraging has deep satisfactions that farming cannot provide.

Some old descriptions of wild edibles say that this plant or that plant is "enjoyed by savages and children," meaning that once you have grown up and got some sense you do not eat this particular thing. We think that if you find something good to eat, either as is or prepared along the lines of one of our recipes, you will be rather proud for having learned something new and a little different. This helps with the mental hurdle.

You may start philosophizing about eating wild. Or, on the other hand, you may get a very real sense of being practical as you gather and cook. Whichever, here is balm for the time-and-place structure which most of us are nudged into.

Above all, we hope you will enjoy the adventure of gourmet tastes that our recipes offer. Far from bare survival, we believe that eating wild offers sensuous delights comparable to other schools of cooking. Simplicity yes, but austerity no. Our wild gourmet wears no hair shirt.

—*MARYANN LASH*

II

I was still a toddler, aged three, when I first became aware of the joys of foraging. I had fallen off a swing, and although my legs didn't hurt, they had reddish stains on them. I licked one of my knees to remove what I thought was blood and uncover what I thought was a wound. Instead I discovered a new taste: delicate, sweet and fruity. I had landed in a patch of wild strawberries. The red fruits were half-hidden under the leaves, but I was in a good position to pick them. I tried a whole berry. It was even better than the juice on my legs. I lay there in the sun and picked and ate. And so I became a confirmed forager.

Cooking naturally follows gathering. Some of the recipes in this book came about as efforts to reward tired gatherers. Anyone baked in the sun for three hours picking little blue beauties deserves a blueberry tart. Other recipes are designed to reveal subtle new tastes. I knew that reindeer browsed raw rock-tripe lichen throughout the Arctic winter. It has a musky, woody essence. Lichen pudding captures it. Cooking and eating motivates lovers of the outdoors to learn more about the edible flora and fauna. A modest helping of sulfur shelf casserole for dinner turned our mycophagist friends into incipient mycologists.

Chokecherry brandy served as an apéritif over ice, sometimes with a little soda water added, can make a pleasant evening gathering memorable. And don't forget, wild edibles are free! A simple lunch of sorrel soup à la Grecque and sourdough bread is not only tasty but economical.

Although my foraging career began serendipitously and intuitively, it developed by apprenticeship. Books like this one got me started and almost took the place of a tutor, but gathering, like small-boat sailing, is better learned from others more experienced.

When I was eight, I would go for walks in the woods with my friend Roger Twitchell, who was a knowledgeable mushroomer. Retired from schoolteaching, he had a farm near us in Washington, Connecticut. Roger wore a French beret, rather baggy large-pocketed pants and a blue-and-white checked shirt; at Christmastime I would tie a bright ribbon around the end of his red Vandyck beard. In the woods we would nibble on snacks of fresh puffballs as we filled our baskets with bright orange and yellow sulfur shelf mushrooms. Unknown specimens went into our empty pockets. We would identify them from guidebooks and a massive, beautifully illustrated encyclopedia that Roger had got when he was a member of the Boston Mycological Club. In one season I learned to identify most of the mushrooms included in *The Wild Gourmet*. I was lucky to have such a teacher; had I grown up in California I might have learned mushrooming from my grandmother who used to gather wild mushrooms by the basketful. At home she would sauté them in butter and place a few specimens in a clean silver spoon for a few minutes. If the spoon blackened she declared the mushrooms "bad" and threw them out. If it didn't, they were "good" and she ate them. The silver-spoon test is totally invalid and unreliable. My grandmother died—in her seventies—of nonmushroom-related causes.

My Swiss father taught my American mother the basics of good Continental cooking. Although my mother did not consider herself a serious cook, her three daughters are. I never did learn how to make brownies like other little girls. Instead, I mastered Roulage Léontine. I then cooked my way through Dione Lucas's *Cordon Bleu Cookbook*, the two-volume *Gourmet Cookbooks*, Louis Diat's *Gourmet Basic French Cookbook* and Julia Child's *Mastering The Art of French Cooking, volumes 1 and 2*. I studied Chinese cooking for two years at The China Institute in New York City. Living in Ethiopia and Italy added new techniques and ideas to my eclectic repertoire.

One early June afternoon in 1972 I was thinning young spinach plants in our neighborhood community garden in Rockport, Massachusetts. MaryAnn was picking the young milkweed buds growing on plants just beyond the cultivated edges of the garden. I told her about a special seasonal treat of Chinese cuisine, to stir-fry the entire young spinach plants in peanut oil with garlic, salt, sugar and pork. The tender green leaves, the slightly bitter red stalk and the crunchy white root of the young plant plus the garlic and pork combine in delicate perfection. It's a dish that shows how the Chinese use complementary colors, tastes and textures. MaryAnn asked some questions about cooking and then introduced me to milkweed buds. That was the first of many conversations that led to this book, which includes only our most successful creations.

One day in mid-July MaryAnn pointed out a chokecherry tree near her house and told me that the fruit would be ripe by the end of August. She would be away. I was to pick as much as I wanted. I returned in August with a pail and picked a quart of dusky red "cherries" without checking their description in any of the guidebooks. I made jelly from them the same day. Later a friend and I sat down to tea and simultaneously sampled small spoonfuls of the jelly only to dash for the nearest sink, choking, gagging and yelling precautions to those nearby. When MaryAnn returned a few days later, I told her about the disaster, dramatizing my painful understanding of how chokecherries got their name. As I described the fruit she looked at me rather strangely. We went to her yard and I pointed to the offending tree. MaryAnn gasped and informed me that I had cooked Weigela. We then picked some shiny, deep purplish-black chokecherries from the adjacent tree. I discovered that while they are somewhat bitter in their raw state, when cooked with sugar and a little water they make a fine jam, syrup or jelly.

This incident serves to remind me that one must always identify any new wilding precisely, so use this book and any of the books listed in our bibliography as references, but if still in doubt, consult an experienced forager. The Audubon Society, colleges (especially extension and adult education divisions), natural history museums and garden clubs often give courses in wild edible identification, or better yet go out and gather (using this book as your guide); sooner or later you will meet experienced foragers in the field.

As you become more aware of the wealth of free food around you, we hope that you will be able to create your own recipes and carry on the art of good cooking and gathering.

—*BABETTE BRACKETT*

January

*J*anuary, not April, is the cruelest month—for the forager, at least. With the turn of the year and the indoor excitement of the holidays behind, the desire to get outdoors can be very strong. But the view from the window is often discouraging; things look terribly bleak.

Keep looking. The Northeast can produce some unexpectedly warm, perhaps sunny, days, known as the January thaw. By all means, take advantage of them and enjoy the first dividend of the returning sun that allows you to prowl around in relative comfort.

On a fine day of January thaw you can get the main ingredients for your drink of the month: hemlock tea. (Socrates did not drink this brew. His hemlock was a poisonous cousin of the parsley family.) As you prepare to head for the woods to find hemlock, remember that while the snow may be melting in sunny places, the shady woodlands will have fair depths of snow.

The bark of the hemlock, as many other tree barks, now may be dark with moisture. The unexpected warmth of the thaw brings out the spicy smell of these different evergreens which provides a promise of fragrant growing times to come, even as the snow crunches underfoot.

Use the second day of thaw, if you are lucky enough to get two in January, for your trip to the sea. The deep blue shadows of the forest are exchanged for a very different blue, or gray-green, or almost black, as the day may bring. But whatever the color of the sea, the dog whelks will be waiting for you.

As you will have to put your hands in cold water, or on cold rocks and kelp, wear gloves. Rubber gloves are best; avoid mittens.

Check a tide table before you go and be ready with a bucket and good warm waterproof boots a half-hour before dead low. This is the ideal time for seaside foraging for intertidal edibles. (Dog whelks are at the high end of the intertidal zone so you do not have to be quite so fussy about dead low as you will have to be with the Irish moss.) At least, try to be at the shore no earlier than one hour before low tide or no later than one after it. Dog whelks are quick picking, so don't postpone your trip for fear of long and bitter exposure to the North Atlantic.

Once back indoors after your foraging forays, the warmth and comfort are again welcome, for they have lost their staleness and now serve to revive your exercised senses and body.

Between expeditions, or if the weather really closes in, try your hand at the following indoor games: in the warmth of your kitchen sprout alfalfa seeds and capture some wild yeasts to make your sourdough starter work.

January (the god Janus) looks two ways. The following recipes will help you look to the time of renewed growth, as you grow your sprouts and sourdough. Although January is hard on foragers, it gives you time to read and dream and make plans for future gathering expeditions.

ALFALFA SEED SPROUTS

Sprinkle 1 tsp. of alfalfa seeds (obtainable at any health or natural food store) into a plastic or glass pint container. Add approximately 2 tbs. of water and cover container with a layer of cheesecloth or plastic screen fastened with a rubber band. Place the container in a dark cupboard for 8 hours. Drain off excess liquid through the cheesecloth or screen covering and gently add 1 to 2 tbs. of water. Tip container to a 45° angle and place upside down in a bowl or on a dish drainer to drain further. Repeat this process 2 times a day for the next 2 to 3 days. Peek at your sprouts now and then and be certain to add enough water so that they won't dry out, but not too much water or they will sit in it and spoil. The sprouts will be ready to eat within 4 to 5 days. Eat them soon or refrigerate them for 2 to 3 days, and start the growing cycle again. The sprouts will grow green leaves if left to sprout in the sunlight rather than a dark closet. One tsp. of dry seed produces 1 cup of mature sprouts.

ALFALFA SEED SPROUT AND SPINACH SALAD

    1 cup fresh alfalfa seed sprouts
    10-oz. pkg. raw spinach leaves, freshly washed,
        tough stems removed, and dried
    5 large mushrooms, cleaned with a damp cloth
        and thinly sliced
    3 scallions, chopped

Toss all ingredients with your favorite dressing, or use French dressing, p. 16a. You may substitute watercress, dandelion greens, lambsquarters, orach, sea lettuce or any favorite green in season. Serves 4.

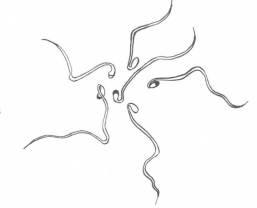

1. Alfalfa Seed Sprouts

FRENCH DRESSING

    1 garlic clove, minced (use a garlic press if available)
    ½ tsp. salt
    10 grinds pepper
    1 tsp. dry mustard powder
    ¼ cup wine vinegar
    ¾ cup olive oil (or a mixture of ¼ cup olive oil
        and ½ cup vegetable oil)

Place the garlic, salt, pepper, mustard and vinegar in a container with a tight-fitting cover, close it and shake until thoroughly blended. Add the oil and shake again. This dressing does not have to be refrigerated.

Variations: Add ¼ tsp. of any of the following herbs to the vinegar mixture: basil, oregano, tarragon, chervil or parsley.

SPROUT SANDWICHES

1 batch of fresh alfalfa sprouts
2 tomatoes, thinly sliced
1 avocado, thinly sliced
1 loaf whole wheat or pumpernickel bread
mayonnaise, salt and pepper to taste

Spread some mayonnaise on a piece of bread. Place 2 slices of tomato, then 2 slices of avocado on it. Season with salt and pepper and sprinkle 1 tbs. of sprouts on top of everything. You can eat it as is, or put another slice of bread on top if you like. Serves 4.

Variation: Make the same sandwich on small rounds of bread or melba toast for a delicious hors d'oeuvre.

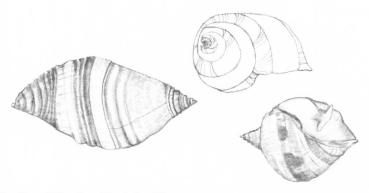

2. Dog Whelk *Thais lapillus*

Dog whelks are found in tide pools or clinging to rocks that are exposed during low tide. Gather the somewhat pear-shaped, meat-filled shells any time of year when they are from 1 to 2 inches long. The color of dog-whelk shells ranges from white or yellow to light brown, either solid color or banded.

DOG WHELK DIP

40 dog whelks, cooked and finely chopped
3 oz. softened cream cheese
2 tbs. sour cream (or more, depending on consistency
    desired)
2 chopped scallions
¼ tsp. curry powder
½ tsp. lemon juice
2 drops Tabasco sauce
salt
pepper

Collect dog whelks at low tide; they cling to the rocks below the high water line. Pick small specimens, no longer than 2 inches. Rinse them in fresh water and boil them for 5 minutes or a few minutes longer if the shells are bigger than 1 inch. Overcooking toughens them. Remove the dog whelk meat from the shells with toothpicks or small skewers. Be certain to discard the flat little brown disk that may still be attached to the meat; it covers the mouth of the shell. Mix the cream cheese and sour cream. Add the dog whelks and the remaining ingredients and salt and pepper to taste. Serve dip with chips, crackers or raw vegetables. Serves 4.

Variation: Substitute periwinkles if dog whelks are not available.

HEMLOCK TEA

1 cup hemlock needles
4 cups boiling water
honey or sugar
lemon

Strip the paler green, newer hemlock needles from the stems and rinse. Warm your teapot while the water is boiling by pouring hot water in it and letting it sit for 1 minute. Pour out the water and place the washed needles inside the teapot. Pour the boiling water over them. Let the tea steep for at least ten minutes, or more if you like yours strong; then pour into teacups and serve with honey or sugar and lemon. Serves 4.

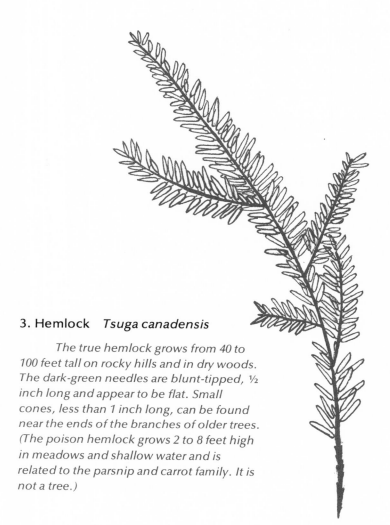

3. Hemlock *Tsuga canadensis*

The true hemlock grows from 40 to 100 feet tall on rocky hills and in dry woods. The dark-green needles are blunt-tipped, ½ inch long and appear to be flat. Small cones, less than 1 inch long, can be found near the ends of the branches of older trees. (The poison hemlock grows 2 to 8 feet high in meadows and shallow water and is related to the parsnip and carrot family. It is not a tree.)

SOURDOUGH WHITE BREAD

Starter

   1 cup milk
   1 cup flour

First make your starter. Keep 1 cup milk at room temperature for 24 hours. Stir in 1 cup flour and cover with cheesecloth until the mixture forms bubbles and smells sour. This takes only 2 to 3 days in the summer and 5 or more in the winter. This starter is a gathering place for all wild yeasts that are living in the air. It can be refrigerated indefinitely when not in regular weekly use; just bring it to room temperature before using. Now that your starter is ready you can begin to make sourdough bread.

Sourdough Bread

 2 cups hot water
 2½ cups white flour
 starter

The night before you plan to make this bread, place all of the starter, 2 cups water and 2½ cups flour in a nonmetal mixing bowl, beat, cover and put in a warm place to ferment overnight.

 2 cups scalded milk
 4 tbs. margarine
 1 pkg. yeast dissolved in ½ cup warm water
 4 tbs. sugar
 1½ tsp. salt
 ½ to 1 tsp. baking soda
 6 to 7 cups unsifted white flour

The next morning put 1½ cups of the fermented batter back in your starter jar to keep it going until you need it again. Drop small cubes of margarine into the scalded milk and let cool to lukewarm. Combine the batter, milk and yeast mixtures and mix well. Combine the sugar, salt and soda, sprinkle over the batter and fold in gently. Add enough flour to make a stiff dough, from 6 to 7 cups. Knead on a floured board until elastic, 5 to 10 minutes. Place the dough in a greased bowl in a warm place. Cover with a damp cloth and let rise until double, about 1 hour. Punch dough down, divide it in half and shape into loaves. Place each loaf in a greased bread pan, butter the top of each loaf, cover with a damp cloth and set in a warm place until double, about 1 hour. Bake at 425° for 10 minutes, reduce heat to 375° and check the loaves after 35 minutes. If they make a hollow sound when tapped, they are done; if not, bake 5 to 10 minutes more and test again. Remove the loaves from their pans and cool on racks for at least 30 minutes. Makes 2 loaves.

Variation: Use 3 cups whole wheat flour and 3 to 4 cups white flour, instead of 6 to 7 cups white flour, for 2 fine whole wheat sourdough loaves.

February

*W*hile January is cruel, February is tough. Maybe, with unconscious wisdom, the calendarmakers assigned this month only 28 days so that we would have a feeling of passing quickly through the vale.

A few fine days of premature warmth as in January may not come in February. But do not despair. As a wild-food forager you will have that extra reason and push to get outside on what otherwise might seem a very unpromising day. Your foraging adventure plans can be the energizer for both adults and children to get out of that frowsty house and clear their lungs.

At this time of year the fields have little to yield. Mainly unprotected from the low temperatures, driving winds and snow of the past months, they are by now pretty well battened down, retrenched, conserving their resources for better days. Life is there, of course, and you will benefit from it in the months ahead.

The sea, on the other hand, continues to provide protection. It moderates and tempers the severest winters, at least as far as temperature goes. While the violence of winter storms on the coast is awesome and wondrous, the water's temperature does not fall at the same rate as that of land and air. You can still go down to the sea, to your intertidal farm once again, and find green goodness for gathering. The storms of winter will provide all ages with the fancy-free, incalculable delights of combing for treasures thrown up on lee shores.

As a result of the wave action on the rocky shore, pieces of Irish moss will be torn off and scattered here and there in clumps. Bleached by rains and possibly dried by the sun if they have been stranded long enough, these clumps have less of the jelling element for blancmange than does fresh Irish moss. If you can get to it (the tide must be at its very lowest if it is an average tide and the sea must be calm) the moss still attached to the rocks is preferred. Setting problems with the blancmange will be less likely if you use this fresh form, which is dark green-brown, sometimes with a purple cast. We like our sea lettuce freshly plucked, too, but this is not crucial; just be sure it is a good bright green.

A plastic or other watertight bucket is always helpful when seashore scavenging because most of your finds will be slippery or slimy. Cut off the narrow tops of 1-gallon plastic bleach or detergent bottles to make handy containers with integrated handles.

After the crispness of your trip, treat yourself to some hot birch tea. Thus the forest will soothe the waves, just as in the summer the sea soothes the land, with its tempering of extremes.

SWEET BIRCH TEA

   2 cups sweet birch twigs cut into half-inch pieces
   4 cups boiling water
   4 lumps of rock candy, or more to taste

Cover the twigs with boiling water and let them steep 10 minutes. Strain the tea into a warmed teapot. Place a piece of rock candy in each teacup and pour the birch tea over it. Serve with sugar and milk if desired. Never boil the twigs, since that will destroy their delicate flavor. Serves 4.

IRISH MOSS BLANCMANGE

   1 cup Irish moss
   4 cups milk
   1 dash salt
   4 tbs. honey, or more as you prefer
   ½ tsp. vanilla

Collect the Irish moss during low tide from rocks and tidal pools.

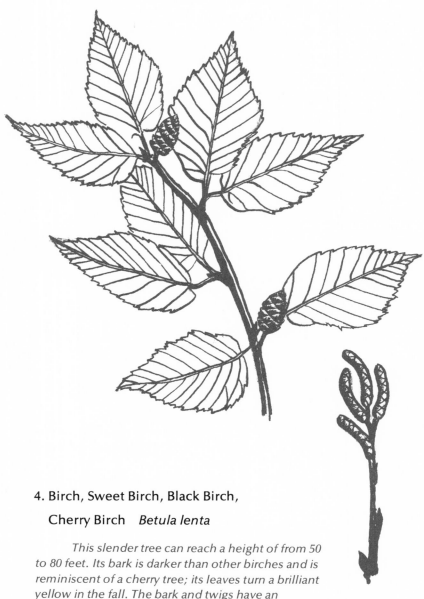

4. Birch, Sweet Birch, Black Birch,
Cherry Birch *Betula lenta*

This slender tree can reach a height of from 50 to 80 feet. Its bark is darker than other birches and is reminiscent of a cherry tree; its leaves turn a brilliant yellow in the fall. The bark and twigs have an unmistakable smell of wintergreen. Catkins usually remain on the ends of the branches throughout winter, long after all the leaves have fallen. Gather the twigs and bark for tea year round; tap the sap from March to April as you would the maple.

26

Wash in at least 2 changes of water. Soak in cold water for 10 minutes. Tie it in cheesecloth and place it with the milk in the top part of a double boiler for about 30 minutes. Stir occasionally. Remove the cheesecloth bag, squeezing excess liquid into the warm milk. Add the salt, honey and vanilla and pour into a serving bowl. Chill until firm (about 3 to 4 hours). Serve plain or with a fruit sauce. Serves 4.

Variations: Add almond, coffee, or chocolate flavoring instead of the vanilla. You can also separate an egg and mix in the yolk when you add the seasonings to the hot milk. Beat the egg white until stiff and fold it gently into the mixture. Refrigerate in a serving bowl until firm.

5. Irish Moss   *Chondrus crispus*

Irish moss forms thick bushy dark-green or reddish-brown mats on rocks intertidally. The tide must be very low to gather it. It gets thrown up on the beach above high tide line during storms and is easier to gather this way in the winter. Irish moss turns white when it is thoroughly dried. Carrageenin, its jelling substance, makes ice cream melt evenly, ink flow smoothly and is used in toothpaste and gelatin.

SEA LETTUCE SOUP

½ cup sea lettuce, dried and chopped
1 tbs. miso paste (available in health-food stores and Japanese
    markets; if unavailable, use 2 beef bouillon cubes)
1 tbs. soy sauce
2 finely chopped scallions

Boil the sea lettuce in 2 cups water for 3 minutes; simmer 20 minutes. Dissolve miso paste in one cup boiling water and combine with sea lettuce and soy sauce. Serve in bowls and sprinkle the scallions on top. Serves 2 to 3.

Variations: Add ½ cup of any cooked vegetable, meat or fish and heat gently 5 minutes.

6. Sea Lettuce   *Ulva lactuca*

The tide does not have to be very low to gather sea lettuce. It is usually attached to rocks or other seaweed—especially Irish moss. Sometimes it floats on the water, trapped in tide pools. Gather the bright green strips of cellophane-like seaweed any time of the year. They are very thin, about 8 to 12 inches long and 2 to 5 inches wide.

HOMEMADE YOGHURT

¼ cup good-quality plain yoghurt
2 cups milk
4 custard cups
1 glass jar with tight-fitting cover

Place 1 tbs. yoghurt in each custard cup. Swirl the yoghurt inside the custard cups so the walls are coated with a thin layer of yoghurt. Bring the milk almost to a boil and allow to cool until you can keep a finger in it for a count of 10. Slowly add ½ cup cooled milk to each custard cup and stir gently to combine the yoghurt culture and milk. Cover the cups with wax paper and put in a warm place for 6 to 8 hours. (In the winter you can simply stick the cups in a cold oven and turn the light on.) The yoghurt should be slightly thickened to the consistency of heavy cream; it may take 2 or 3 hours longer if the place is not warm enough. Place 3 of the covered custard cups in the refrigerator where the yoghurt will continue to thicken. Pour the contents of the fourth cup into the glass jar. Screw the top on tightly and refrigerate. When you begin a new batch of yoghurt use the yoghurt from the jar to coat the custard cups. Always return the contents of one custard cup to a clean glass jar to keep the culture working. Serves 3.

Variations: Use skim instead of regular milk, or a combination of powdered skim milk and regular milk for a low-calorie yoghurt.

YOGHURT AND CUCUMBER SALAD

2 cucumbers, peeled and sliced
1 small clove garlic
¼ tsp. salt
1 cup yoghurt
½ tsp. dried mint leaves

Mash the garlic with the salt and add the yoghurt. Pour the dressing over the cucumbers and garnish with dried mint. Serves 4.

March

$\mathcal{T}$hough we start the year with January, March is truly our first month, our month of wonder, for the wheel of the year does not turn steadily but rather gathers its energies for wavelike changes. We may sense the changes fairly early in March, or we may be tantalized until nearly the end of the month. With the purification or sacrificial aspect of February behind us, having passed through the test successfully, we can with some instinctive sense of accomplishment march into March. The sugar bush with its sweetness awaits us.

Maples, of course, will not have leaves now for quick and easy identification. Check the silhouette in the drawing (Figure 10) and remember that the skeletal shape of the maple tree is very similar to its leaf outline: generally broad and symmetrical, with rhythmic points. The bark of the mature sugar maple is somewhat shaggy. The Norway maple, which you could use, has a smoother and grayer trunk. Swamp maples produce a good sap, too.

The art in sapping is in choosing the right time to tap. Warm days and cold nights are necessary to get and keep the sap running. It will not run well when above 50° Fahrenheit or below 32°. You must catch those 3 to 4 weeks (some years only 2 weeks or less) which produce a good run.

Though it may seem a little involved at first, once you run through it the process is quite simple.

Gather a brace and bit less than ½ inch in diameter, a sharp knife, light watertight 1-gallon pails with handles, a hammer, nails and a roll of aluminum foil.

When you have spotted a fairly mature maple (with a trunk at least 35 inches in circumference), drill a hole 2 inches deep on its south side, about 5 feet from the ground. Cut a 3- to 5-inch-long tapered wooden spout and hollow out a V-shaped channel in it for the sap to run along. You may find sumacs or birches handy trees from which to make the spouts. (Some hardware stores sell metal spouts.) Hammer the spout into the hole you've made in the tree; it should fit tightly or the sap will not run down the channel. If you taste the sap as it drips off the channel you may find it slightly sweetish. It will seem watery if you think of your goal of thick syrup. Drive a nail into the tree a few inches above the spout, for hanging the pail. Make a cover of aluminum foil to keep rain, sleet, snow and little black bugs out of the sap and—just let it flow.

Collect the sap daily and boil it down to 1/30 of its original volume. As it reduces watch it constantly. The process speeds up toward the end and it is very easy to burn an unattended batch.

In a small gently moving stream, on a dark and windy day in late March, we were lucky enough to find more watercress than we ever dreamed of. Like Ophelia's tresses, it swayed with the current. (If the stream looked muddy or in any way polluted, we would soak our watercress in 4 drops of Chlorox dissolved in 2 quarts of water.) We used it to garnish soups, in herb butters on sourdough toast, with lichens and chili; we stopped our watercress orgy only at dessert and coffee.

The fields of March, unlike those of February, yield small reddish clumps of dandelions. Best, we believe, to avoid digging dandelion roots in lawns where there may have been an application of weed killer; we dug roots on the edges of fields. We came upon a bayberry plant with some of its dried brown leaves lingering on the branches. Early settlers called it the candleberry because they steeped wax from its fruits to make their candles.

March helps get you in shape for even more active foraging to come. The stage is set.

7. Bayberry, Bay Laurel *Myrica pennsylvanica*

The bayberry grows in seacoast areas and inland on rocky, dry soils, where it ranges from 1 to 5 feet high. Crush the dark-green leaves and smell their unmistakable aroma. The fruits, or berries, appear in the summer and are grayish blue, waxy and as aromatic as the leaves. While dried leaves can be collected from the bush throughout the winter, the best time to collect and dry bay laurel is in early summer when the new leaves are formed. Wash and spread the leaves on a screen or tray and dry them in the sun or attic; store the completely dry leaves in airtight containers.

BAY LAUREL CHILI

2 tbs. bacon drippings
2 to 5 tsp. chili powder, depending on how hot you like it
1 large onion, chopped
2 cloves garlic, minced
1 to 2 lbs. hamburger
2 cups canned tomatoes (16-oz. can)
4 cups canned kidney beans (28-oz. can)
1 tsp. salt
5 grinds pepper
4 to 6 bay laurel leaves
1 tsp. sugar

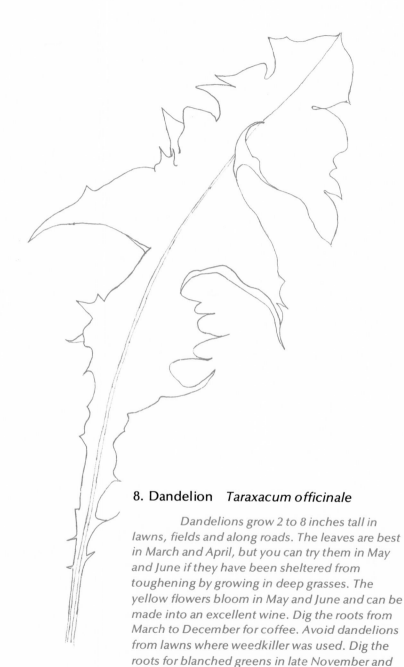

8. Dandelion *Taraxacum officinale*

Dandelions grow 2 to 8 inches tall in lawns, fields and along roads. The leaves are best in March and April, but you can try them in May and June if they have been sheltered from toughening by growing in deep grasses. The yellow flowers bloom in May and June and can be made into an excellent wine. Dig the roots from March to December for coffee. Avoid dandelions from lawns where weedkiller was used. Dig the roots for blanched greens in late November and in December.

Although the best time to pick bay leaves is in early summer when the new leaves are formed, you should now be able to find plenty of naturally dried leaves still clinging to the branches. Sauté the onion and chili powder in the melted bacon drippings for 10 minutes. Add hamburger and cook until brown. Add the remaining ingredients, cover the pot and cook over low heat for 1 hour. Correct seasonings to taste and serve. Serves 4 to 6.

DANDELION COFFEE

¼ cup dandelion roots
2 tsp. chocolate bits
2 tbs. rum

Wash and scrub the dandelion roots you have dug, to remove all dirt. Dry the roots thoroughly and roast in a 250° oven for 2 to 4 hours, until they are brittle and dark brown inside. Grind them and use the powder to make 4 cups of coffee. A drip pot with filter paper is recommended. Add the 2 tsp. chocolate bits, 2 tbs. rum and serve after dinner. Serves 4.

SAUTÉED LICHEN AND WATERCRESS

3 cups rock-tripe lichen, washed
1½ cups watercress, washed
1 scallion, minced
5 tbs. butter
¼ tsp. salt
4 grinds pepper

Melt the butter in a skillet over medium heat. Add the lichen, watercress and scallion and stir for 3 minutes. Add the salt and pepper and serve immediately. This vegetable dish goes well with beef, chicken or fish and can even be part of a Chinese meal. Serves 4.

MAPLE SAUCE FOR CRÊPES

4 gal. maple sap
¼ cup chopped black walnuts

Place sap in a big kettle and bring to a boil. Keep it boiling gently and stir occasionally until it forms a thick syrup, at about 1/30 of its original volume. Watch the syrup carefully in the last stages. If it is boiling too fast throw in some cubes of butter to slow down the bubbling. The sauce will change from clear to light brown. Four gallons of sap should produce about 2 cups of syrup. The syrup must be refrigerated to keep. Take ½ cup or more, warm it gently and add the chopped nuts. Serve over the crêpes. Serves 4.

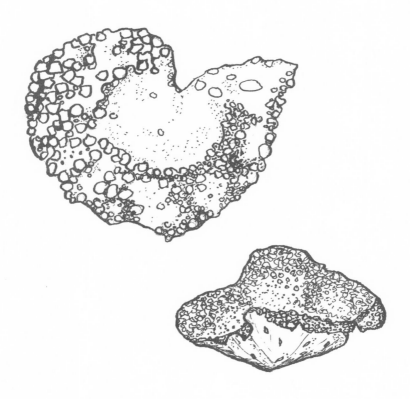

9. Lichen, Rock-tripe *Umbilicaria*

These dark-gray pockmarked leathery blisters are attached to rocks from a central point. They become olive and brown colored when wet, and grow from 1 to 4 inches in diameter, looking like small elephants' ears. This lichen is available for picking year round in shady, rocky woodland areas.

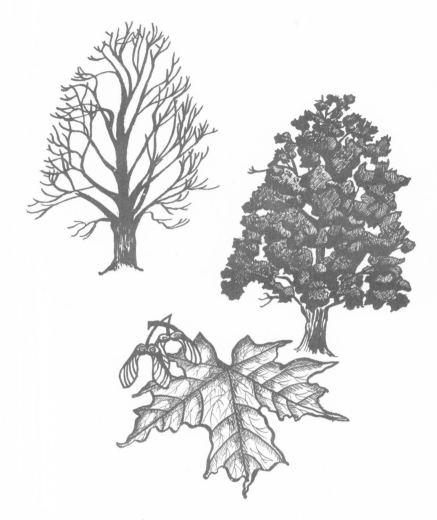

10. Maple   *Acer saccharum*

Locate sugar maples in the spring, summer and fall by the unmistakable shape of their leaves, which glow with brilliant reds, oranges and yellows during the fall. Mature maples can grow from 75 to 120 feet and their gray-brown bark becomes somewhat shaggy. They prosper in any soil and are commonly found in open areas and along the edges of woods. Sap runs from the first thaw until the leaf buds burst. It cannot run below 32° Fahrenheit or above 50° Fahrenheit, so you must catch those 3 to 4 sugaring weeks, possibly in February, generally in March, or even in April if spring comes late.

CRÊPES

1 cup flour
3 tbs. sugar
¼ tsp. salt
3 eggs, beaten
½ cup milk
½ cup cream
1 tsp. vanilla or orange extract, or 1 tbs. rum or other liqueur

Sift the flour, salt and sugar into the beaten eggs and mix. Add the remaining liquids and stir until smooth. Don't beat the batter too much or the crêpes will be tough. Let the batter rest in the refrigerator for 1 to 2 hours. Heat a heavy skillet or crêpe pan over medium high heat and brush with a thin coating of butter. Ladle 2 tbs. of batter in the center and quickly tilt the skillet so that the batter spreads out to form a round crêpe approximately 5 inches in diameter. Check to see if the bottom is brown after 1½ minutes. Turn the crêpe when browned and cook the other side. Fold or roll the cooked crêpe and place on a warm serving platter. Cover the crêpe platter with aluminum foil and keep in a warm oven (150° to 180°F) while you continue cooking the rest of the batter. Serves 4.

11. Watercress   *Nasturtium officinale*

The smooth dark-green leaves of watercress are attached to 5- to 9-inch long strands which form a clump. Gather watercress from March to December from the beds of shallow brooks and streams of moving water. If there is any question about whether or not the water is polluted, soak the cress in a solution of 4 drops Chlorox dissolved in 2 quarts water.

WATERCRESS BUTTER

    ¼ lb. butter
    2 tbs. chopped wild watercress
    1 tbs. chopped parsley
    1 tbs. chopped chives or scallions
    salt and pepper (optional)

Cream the butter. Add the finely chopped greens and mix
thoroughly. Put the mixture in a serving crock or bowl or form it
into a roll, and refrigerate. Serve it on toast or crackers as an hors
d'oeuvre. Serves 4 to 6.

Variation: Add 1 to 2 tsp. of grated Sap Sago cheese to the mixture
before chilling it.

WATERCRESS SOUP

    2 cups wild watercress
    2 medium potatoes
    3 tbs. butter
    1 qt. chicken broth
    1 medium onion, finely chopped
    1 bay laurel leaf
    ½ tsp. salt
    5 grinds pepper
    ¼ tsp. paprika (optional)
    ¼ cup heavy cream
    1 egg yolk

Thoroughly wash the watercress and chop it fine. Peel and dice
the potatoes. Melt the butter and add the watercress, onion and
bay laurel leaf. Sauté 5 minutes or until the watercress is wilted.
Add the potatoes, chicken broth, salt, pepper and paprika and
cook 20 minutes. Beat the egg yolk and cream together, and warm
by adding 1 cup of the hot soup; pour the egg and cream mixture
into the soup, stir, and serve at once. Sprinkle chopped
watercress on top of each serving as a garnish. Serves 4 to 6.

April

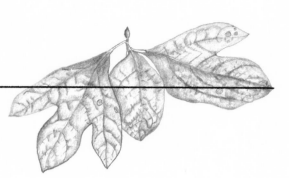

*A*pril is a fantastic month, and, likewise, we in New England tend to have fantasies about April. The iron grip of winter has been broken; we see our world daily turning toward growth and greenness. We become impatient, too, as is the way of human nature. Surely, if this miracle can happen, any miracle is possible. Why, we demand, is not April warmer, less muddy, more perfect?

As we walk and forage in April, we can find satisfaction enough in what the new season provides. We become rooted in the reality of the fresh juicy greens miraculously available. We find sufficient delight for all our impatient demands. We see our foraging basket filling with a greater variety of edibles than winter's supply of interesting additions to our storebought groceries.

As you pick leaves from patches of sheep sorrel, note their locations for collecting them during the rest of the spring, summer and even fall. This you will start doing automatically, making mental notes, or even small maps, of where particular plants can be found. For instance, a plant may be easier to identify in flower than when it is fruiting, yet often it is the fruit you are after. Identifying the plant in flower will help you remember where it lives for gathering later.

We found the first delicate leaves of wild carrots in many of the fields we walked across this month. In April we use the plant in its "carrot form," that is, the root; in summer we know it as Queen Anne's Lace, its flower form, which is more familiar and a little

12. Wild Carrot, Queen Anne's Lace *Daucus carota*

Wild carrots grow in waysides and fields and on dry waste land. Look for the hairy-stemmed, yellowish-green, much-divided and subdivided leaves in April and May. Dig up the small white roots underneath and smell their unmistakable carrot scent. Whitish flat-topped clusters of flowers with a single purple flower in the center bloom 2 to 3 feet high from June to September. The old flowers fold up on themselves when dry, for which they are named "birds' nests." Gather carrot seed clusters on a windy day in September or October; rub the seeds between your fingers so the chaff blows away and the cleaned seeds fall onto a plate or paper.

easier to identify. Do not forget its location, for in September it provides edible seeds. Take time to identify it carefully, so as not to confuse it with the poisonous hemlock, which has purple spots on its stems.

One of the earliest new growths is that of the day lily shoots and tubers. To get the tubers, carefully dig up the whole plant. This helps to thin the clumps and will be good for the remaining plants. You might like to bring a few plants home to your own garden for food and for midsummer beauty right at your door. Unlike many wildings, they are as tough and prolific in your garden as in the fields.

Again we return to the sea, this time for mussels and at low tide. We found a rich harvest under rockweed fronds and in cracks in the rocks of the tidal pools. Mussels cling tenaciously by their threads to the rocks, so you must yank them hard. Fortunately, mussels are still largely overlooked as food in this country; you can find good-sized ones in great quantities.

Juicy green sprouts, very much like asparagus, are April's real miracle, we believe. These sprouts are the first growth above ground of the fiddleheads of the ferns. Growing in most wooded, or edge of woods, damp places, they confirm that spring is on its way. Like the new lambs in the fields, their tightly furled croziers confront any doubters with irrefutable evidence. The fiddleheads are the symbol of April for us, and April is truly a month of symbols.

WILD CARROTS

    2 cups wild carrots, peeled and washed
    2 tbs. butter
    3 tbs. brown sugar or honey or a mixture of both
    ½ tsp. salt
    2 tbs. apple or orange juice

Dig the carrots where last year's Queen Anne's Lace flowered. Cut the carrots into 1-inch pieces and sauté them in the butter over medium heat for 10 minutes. Add the remaining ingredients, cover tightly and let the mixture cook over low heat for 20 minutes. Taste and correct seasonings if necessary. If the carrots are still a bit too crunchy, cook them 10 minutes longer. (Sometimes the carrot core remains too tough to eat. It can be slipped out easily with a chopstick or any blunt-tipped object.) Serves 4.

STIR-FRIED DANDELION GREENS AND PORK

1 lb. young washed dandelion greens, 4 to 6 cups
4 tbs. peanut oil
1 minced clove garlic
¼ cup water
½ tsp. salt
¼ tsp. sugar
2 1-inch thick center-cut pork chops, frozen for
 1 hour, then cut in slices ⅛-inch thick
1 tbs. soy sauce (Chinese or Japanese, if available)
1 tbs. sherry
1 tsp. cornstarch

Marinate the sliced pork in soy sauce, sherry and cornstarch. Clean the dandelion greens. Heat 2 tbs. peanut oil in a large heavy iron skillet over high heat for 20 seconds. Add garlic and stir rapidly for 10 seconds. Add greens and stir constantly so that each green is coated with a little oil and doesn't burn. Add salt, sugar and water, stir, then cover skillet, turning heat to medium to let the greens steam. Stir after 1 minute and steam 1 to 3 minutes more, depending on their age and tenderness. Remove the greens and water to a serving dish. Heat 2 tbs. peanut oil in the same skillet over high heat for 30 seconds. Add the marinated pork slices and stir constantly until every piece turns from pink to white, about 2 to 4 minutes. Combine the cooked greens and pork in the skillet and heat for 30 seconds, always stirring. If there is too much liquid in the skillet, make a thin paste of 1 tsp. cornstarch dissolved in 1 tbs. water. Add the paste to the skillet mixture, stir, and remove from heat when the sauce is thick and shiny. Serve with boiled rice. Serves 4.

Variation: Fry 3 slices of fresh ginger root in the hot peanut oil with the sliced pork. Remove the ginger before you add the cooked greens.

DANDELION WINE

3 qts. dandelion blossoms
 (be certain they are yellow, fully open and dry)
4 qts. boiling water

3 lbs. sugar
2 lemons
1 orange
1 yeast cake

Collect the dandelions as early in the day as possible because it takes quite a while for the mixture to cool to 100°. Pour the boiling water over the blossoms. Let the mixture stand 3 hours; do not stir it. Strain the mixture into a big cooking pot and add the sugar and the lemon and orange rinds. Cook over medium heat for 15 minutes. Cut up the orange and lemons and place them in a 2-gal. crock, jar or plastic pail. Pour the cooked mixture on top of the fruit. When the mixture cools to 100° (a little warmer than body temperature), add the yeast which has been dissolved in 1 cup of the warm mixture, then add the rest of the mixture. Let it stand 12 hours and strain it once again. Return the mixture to the crock, cover and let it stand 2 months. Strain into bottles and sample it in 6 months.

SCALLOPED DAY LILY SHOOTS AND TUBERS

2 cups day lily tubers, peeled and washed
2 to 3 cups day lily shoots
2 tbs. butter
2 tbs. flour
1½ cups hot milk
1 tsp. salt
4 grinds pepper
¼ cup grated Parmesan cheese
¼ cup buttered bread crumbs

Boil the tubers and shoots for 5 minutes. Drain and chop into small pieces. Melt butter over medium heat and stir in the flour for 1 minute. Add the hot milk, salt and pepper, and stir until thickened. Put the chopped shoots and tubers in a greased 1½-qt. casserole and cover with the white sauce. Combine the grated cheese and bread crumbs and sprinkle on top. Bake in a 350° oven for 20 minutes or until the top is nicely browned. Serves 4.

Variation: Add ¼ tsp. ground mustard to the sauce.

13. Day Lily *Hemerocallis fulva*

The light-orange upward-facing flowers open for just a day, but there are many unopened buds to supply a constant source of flowers during July and August. The long, thin green leaves look like bent swords. Day lilies grow along roads and open areas with well-drained soil. Cut the young green shoots in April. Dig up the entire plant and remove some of the tubers from April to November.

45

CREAMED FIDDLEHEADS

1 lb. fiddleheads
2 cups water
½ tsp. salt
5 grinds pepper
butter to taste (approximately 1 tbs.)

Pick the fiddleheads when they are no bigger than 8 inches tall; break them off as far down as they are tender. Pull each fiddlehead through your hands in order to remove all their furry surface hairs. Wash and tie them together in bunches like asparagus. Bring 2 cups of salted water to a boil and cook them until tender, approximately 10 to 20 minutes. Drain and season them with salt, pepper and butter. Serve them plain or with a cream sauce.

Cream Sauce

3 tbs. butter
2 tbs. flour
½ cup milk and ½ cup cream, mixed
½ tsp. salt
3 grinds pepper (use white rather than black if available)
2 pinches nutmeg (freshly grated if possible)

Melt the butter over medium heat and stir in flour for 1 minute. Add the milk and cream mixture and stir constantly until thickened. Add seasonings and spoon sauce over the cooked fiddleheads. Serves 4.

RICE WITH MUSSELS

1 pt. mussels
1 tsp. lemon juice
2 tbs. olive oil
2 cloves garlic
1 tbs. chopped parsley
¼ tsp. saffron
1 tsp. salt
5 grinds pepper
1 cup rice
2½ cups mussel broth

Scrub the mussels, debeard them and boil in 2 cups water for 5 minutes. Save the liquid. Remove the cooked mussels from their shells and sprinkle 1 tsp. lemon juice over them. Strain the reserved broth through cheesecloth and measure it. If you do not have 2½ cups liquid you can add bottled clam juice, fish stock or water. Sauté the garlic, parsley and saffron in olive oil for 3 minutes. Add the rice and cook 2 more minutes, stirring constantly. Add the mussel broth and bring it to a quick boil. Cover and cook on low heat for 20 minutes. Add the mussels and cook for 5 to 10 more minutes or until all the broth is absorbed. This dish can be kept covered in a warm oven for 1 or 2 hours before eating. It goes particularly well with fish or chicken. Serves 4 to 6.

14. Fiddlehead Ostrich Fern *Matteuccia struthiopteris*
Bracken Fern *Pteridium aquilinum*

The small young green fiddleheads of the fern are covered with soft woolly brown fuzz if they are ostrich ferns or silvery silken fuzz if they are bracken. They grow along streams and other moist places in woods and semishaded areas. Pick them when they are only 4 to 8 inches tall. Because they are easy to miss when this size (in April and early May), look for last year's brown, dead stalks.

CREAM OF MUSSEL SOUP

40 to 50 mussels, cleaned and debearded
1 cup dry white wine
1 large onion, finely chopped
2 tbs. butter
2 tbs. flour
1 cup warm milk
1 cup cream
1 tsp. salt
5 grinds pepper
2 tbs. finely chopped parsley

Place the mussels and wine in a saucepan, bring to a boil and simmer 5 minutes until they open. Strain the liquid through a layer of cheesecloth to remove any dirt, and reserve the broth. Remove the mussels from their shells and chop them. Sauté the onions in melted butter for 3 minutes. Add the flour and stir for 1 minute. Pour in the warm milk and mussel broth and bring almost to a boil, stirring constantly. Add the parsley, mussels, salt, pepper and cream, heat for 1 more minute and serve immediately. Don't let the soup boil, or the mussels will toughen. Serves 4.

Variations: You may prefer to leave the mussels whole, especially if they are small. You can also add 1 cup cooked rice or diced potato for a heartier version.

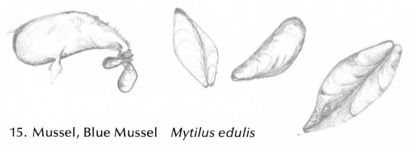

15. Mussel, Blue Mussel   *Mytilus edulis*

The tide has to be fairly low for musselling. The blue-black shells should be 2 to 5 inches long, tightly clamped to rocks by their black threadlike beards. Sometimes they are hidden under layers of rockweed. Do not gather mussels that live in mud flats or that are unattached to rocks. Collect mussels in any season, but be certain that they are growing in an unpolluted, well-washed coast, free from red tide or manmade disasters.

16. Sassafras *Sassafras albidum*

The green bark on the twigs of sassafras trees and saplings makes winter and early spring identification a little easier. The rest of the year, look for combinations of leaves that are oval, mitten-shaped or even two-thumbed. Look for 2- to 6-foot saplings and 20- to 90-foot trees in dry woods and thickets. Gather the leaves from April to September and dig the roots year round.

SASSAFRAS TEA

⅓ cup sassafras root
4 cups water
Sugar or honey to taste

Pull up a few young sassafras saplings and cut off their roots. (Dry the young leaves for gumbo.) Scrub the roots well and scrape them if necessary to remove the dirt. Place the roots in an enamel or stainless-steel saucepan. Cover the roots with water and bring to a boil. Simmer at least 10 minutes, then taste if the tea is strong enough. If not, keep simmering and tasting every 5 minutes until the tea is right. It should be a dusty pink color. Serve the hot tea with sugar or honey for a refreshing spring drink. Dry or freeze the boiled roots and make tea from them 2 or 3 more times before gathering new ones. Serves 4.

Variation: Sassafras tea is also very good chilled. It has a refreshing root-beer-like taste that children especially like.

SHEEP SORREL SOUP

4 cups sheep sorrel
2 tbs. butter
2 tbs. rice or pastina
4 cups chicken broth
½ tsp. salt
3 grinds pepper
1 tsp. sugar

You can add cut-up lettuce or spinach leaves to the sorrel if you can't find four cupfulls. Wash greens and cook in melted butter for 10 minutes. Add the remaining ingredients and cook slowly until the rice or pastina is tender, about 15 minutes. Pour soup in blender and blend until ingredients are puréed. Taste, adjust seasonings if necessary and serve. Garnish soup with a fresh sorrel leaf or a thin slice of lemon. Serves 6.

17. Sheep Sorrel

Rumex acetosella

The dark-green arrowhead-shaped leaves of sorrel become tinged with red in the fall; they have a subtle lemony taste. Sorrel grows from 4 to 12 inches high on open places everywhere, though it does especially well in dry, acid soils. The green or reddish-brown flower heads rise 1 to 5 inches above the edible leaves. Gather sorrel from April to October.

May

*J*f you are fairly new to discovering and using wild edibles, May is a month of learning, searching and finding. You might want to check one or more of the books listed in the bibliography, as well as this month's drawings and descriptions of plants. There are many adventures in May, and the more you know, the more there is to enjoy. No detailed, scientific botany is necessary. May's edibles, like all those chosen here for your foraging, have real character. They do not suffer from the herd look. You will not have to worry about confusing them with inedible look-alikes.

May will take you to field and stream, into woodlands and the edges of woods. May will give you many excuses to follow the bluebird, which returns to New England this month. May is both the pride of perfection, and the luxury of more to come. May is a sudden bright burst to New England eyes accustomed to the cool grays, blues and browns of lingering winter. We always feel a little like the mole at the feast for the first few perfect days.

Molelike or not, we can start to forage new additions for salads: young chicory leaves, wild garlic, onions, chives, wild lettuce and even violets. We gathered young cattail shoots when they were about 2 feet high during a walk along a brackish marsh near the ocean, and peeled and ate a few of the stalks right on the spot. The edges of freshwater ponds also yielded a good supply of cattails later in the month.

18. Wild Asparagus

Asparagus officinalis

It is quite easy to locate wild asparagus in the summer when the light-green hairlike branches extend from the mature 3-foot-high plants, which grow in open areas with good, rich soil. Otherwise, look for last year's brown, dead stalks complete with side branches but no fine hairs, rising 3 feet above the young light-green sprouts in May. Cut the asparagus at ground level when the sprouts are 6 to 10 inches high and the tips are still tightly closed.

52

Once while walking in an old apple orchard we were overjoyed to find a crop of morel mushrooms. Sometimes farmers will burn the land in old orchards and around elm trees to induce growth of these delectable mushrooms. But we saw no signs of burnt-over land, just the unmistakable brainlike convolutions of one of New England's choicest spring mushrooms. You will have to wait for late summer and early fall for the other mushrooms we recommend as foolproof.

Wild asparagus, usually an escapee from some cultivated plot, is truly worth the search. You can find it now on first go, but if you are not a natural Sherlock Holmes it is easier to spot the mature fronds in August, September and October and remember to go back in May. During May the weathered stalks of last year's crop may help you locate the sites of this year's new shoots.

Also in the truly delectable shoot group is the early stage of the poke plant. These shoots are like nothing else. You will want to use all the poke shoots you can find on the edges of woodlands and in open places. At their best when just poking up through the dead leaves, they should not be used after their leaves have started to unfurl.

Finally, we can toast and thank May with fragrant mint tea and so forever associate the warmth and smell of mint with May's perfection. You can, if you like, remember May all year round by drying some mint leaves on trays in your attic or furnace room or any warm, dry place and storing them in airtight containers. Make the tea the same way whether you use fresh or dried mint leaves. Red and white clover blossoms can also be picked and dried from May through September.

STIR-FRIED WILD ASPARAGUS

    1 bunch (3 to 4 cups) wild asparagus,
        cut into 1-inch pieces
    2 tbs. peanut oil
    ¼ cup chicken broth or water
    1 tsp. salt
    ¼ tsp. sugar
    1 tsp. cornstarch dissolved in 1 tbs. water

Wash the asparagus carefully. You need not peel the stalks if you have broken them off at the point of least resistance. Heat a heavy iron skillet for 30 seconds over high heat. Then add the oil and swirl it around for 30 seconds more. Add the asparagus pieces and stir constantly until each piece is coated with oil, approximately 2 minutes. Add the chicken broth or water, salt and sugar and cover tightly to let it steam for 2 minutes. Taste a piece and if it seems too crunchy, cover and steam 1 more minute. (Remember that Chinese-style vegetables should be firmer than the usual American style.) Give the cornstarch mixture a quick stir, add it to the asparagus and stir rapidly for 20 seconds or so until the sauce is thick and shiny. Remove it from heat and serve immediately. Serves 4.

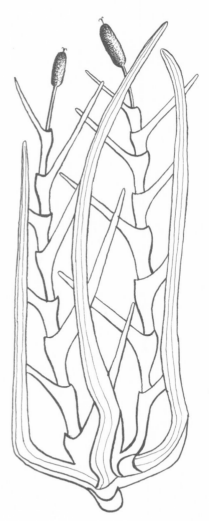

19. Cattail
Typha latifolia

Yellow flowers bloom at the end of the brownish stalks for a short time in the spring and then turn into the brown cattails which give this familiar plant its name. Look for its light-green swordlike leaves and its brown stalks growing 4 to 8 feet high along marsh and pond borders. Gather the shoots in May and June and the cattails in August and September.

STEAMED CATTAIL STALKS

40 cattail stalks about 5 inches long
2 tbs. butter
½ tsp. salt
3 grinds pepper

Remove the tough outer green leaves from the cattail stalks and use only the white part which looks somewhat like the bulb end of a scallion. If you don't have a steaming basket you can improvise in the following way. Take an old tuna fish can and cut off both ends. Place it in the bottom of a pot and add water to within 1 inch of the top of the can. Find a heatproof dish with slightly sloping sides that will fit inside the pot and allow 1 inch of space between it and the sides of the pot; put on top of the tuna fish can. Place the cattails, butter and seasonings in the dish and bring the water to a boil. Cover the pot and keep on medium heat to sustain the boil; check every 10 minutes or so to be certain that the water doesn't boil away. The cattails should be ready in 20 to 30 minutes. Use pot-holders when removing the hot dish from the pot. Serves 4.

Variations: Serve the cattails with a simple white sauce, a cheese sauce or a hollandaise.

NORTHERN GUMBO

4 pieces of bacon, diced
1 small onion, diced
1 green pepper, diced
1 cup green beans, diced
½ cup rice
3 tomatoes, skinned and seeded
4 cups chicken broth
1 tsp. salt
¼ tsp. pepper
¼ tsp. paprika
¼ tsp. Tabasco sauce
1 cup baby shrimp
½ cup diced chicken
1 tsp. powdered sassafras leaves
    (sometimes called filé powder)

Dry young sassafras leaves in a 200° oven for 2 hours. Crush them into powder in a mortar and store in an airtight container. Cook the bacon in a 2-qt. saucepan over medium heat for 5 minutes. Add the onion and green pepper to the bacon and sauté for 5 minutes. Add the rice, green beans, tomatoes, broth, Tabasco sauce and seasonings. Bring to a boil, turn heat to low, cover and cook for 20 minutes. Add the shrimp, chicken and powdered sassafras. Cook for 2 minutes, being careful not to boil the gumbo. Taste and correct the seasonings if necessary. This hearty soup is great for lunch. Serves 4.

Variations: Add ½ to ¾ cup more rice and the gumbo becomes an entrée. Make up your own version by adding leftover meat, fish or vegetables.

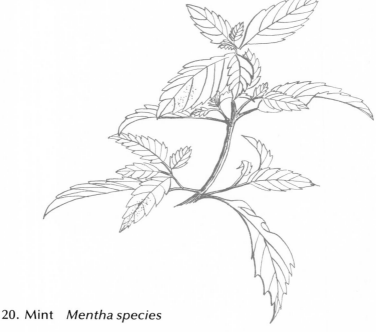

20. Mint *Mentha species*

The mint plant has somewhat hairy dark-green leaves that give off a strong mint scent when crushed. In midsummer tiny white or purple flowers grow in a circle at the junction of the leaf and square-shaped plant stem. Look for mint growing from 10 to 18 inches tall in wet places and along the edges of fields from May to September. Many varieties of mint grow on their own; water mint, spearmint and peppermint can be found along the edges of lawns and places where cultivated herb gardens might have been.

56

MINT TEA

2½ tbs. fresh or dried chopped mint leaves
1 qt. water
4 tsp. honey

Bring the water to a boil and pour it over the leaves. Let the tea steep for at least five minutes and serve with a tsp. of honey in each cup. Serves 4.

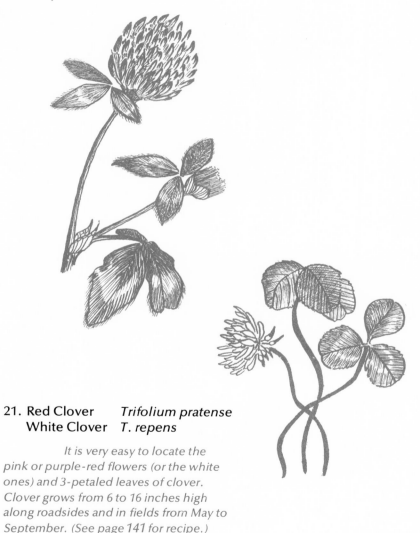

21. Red Clover   *Trifolium pratense*
    White Clover   *T. repens*

It is very easy to locate the pink or purple-red flowers (or the white ones) and 3-petaled leaves of clover. Clover grows from 6 to 16 inches high along roadsides and in fields from May to September. (See page 141 for recipe.)

SAUTÉED MORELS ON TOAST

1 lb. morels
4 to 6 tbs. butter
salt and pepper to taste

Pick only the freshest and firmest morels. Don't ever bother with the somewhat caved-in brownish ones. Brush off the excess dirt and carefully rinse them in cold water to remove remaining dirt. Drain them on absorbent towels. Slice each morel down the middle and sauté in butter for 30 minutes over low heat. Gently season with a little salt and pepper and serve on freshly toasted sourdough white bread. Serves 4 to 6.

Variation: After the first 15 minutes of sautéing add 1 cup of dry sherry and simmer until the liquid is almost evaporated. Stir in ½ cup cream, lightly season with salt and pepper, and serve on toast. Either recipe goes well with roast beef, chicken or fish.

22. Morel   *Morchella esculenta*

The conical, pitted, ridged cap surface of the morel looks somewhat like tripe. The caps are tan or brown, the stems lighter colored; both are hollow and the flesh is brittle. Morels grow 2 to 6 inches tall, with ½- to 1-inch-thick stems, in old apple orchards, burned-over ground and under elm trees. Look for morels in May when oak leaves are at the mouse-ear stage of expansion.

23. Poke shoot
Phytolacca americana

Pokeweed is also known as inkberry because of its clusters of deep-purple juicy berries in the fall; birds have been known to become intoxicated after eating them. Locate the coarse reddish stems in the summer in fields, roadsides and the edges of woods when the mature plant reaches 6 to 8 feet in height, and return for the shoots the following spring. Or look for the tall old dead stalks in April; the shoots will be nearby. Gather the shoots from April to early June before the young leaves start to unfold. The large root is a violent emetic and is sometimes used as a substitute for ipecac, so be sure to use only the green shoots.

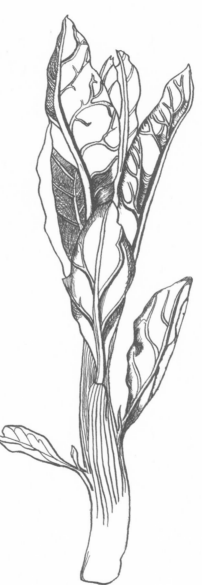

POKEWEED SHOOTS AND CHICKEN

4 cups pokeweed shoots
1 tbs. peanut oil
¾ tsp. salt
¼ tsp. sugar
1 cup chicken broth
2 chicken breasts, boned and cut into
    ½-inch cubes (simmer the bones in 1½ cups water
    for 1 hour to make the broth)
1 tbs. soy sauce
1 tbs. sherry
1 tsp. cornstarch
2 tbs. peanut oil
2 tbs. cornstarch completely dissolved in 3 tbs. water

Wash and cut the poke shoots diagonally into 1-inch pieces. Combine the cut-up chicken, soy sauce, sherry and 1 tsp. cornstarch in a bowl; stir to coat each chicken piece with the marinade and save for later. Heat a heavy iron skillet or wok for 30 seconds over high heat. Add the 1 tbs. oil and swirl it around for 30 seconds more, making certain that the entire cooking surface is coated. Add the poke shoots and stir constantly until each piece is coated with oil, approximately 2 minutes. Add the salt, sugar and broth, cover tightly and let it steam for 2 minutes. Remove the pokeweed shoots to a serving dish and heat 2 tbs. oil in the skillet or wok. Add the marinated cubed chicken breasts and cook over high heat, stirring constantly until done, approximately 5 minutes. Pour the cooked pokeweed shoots back into the skillet with the chicken, stir and add the cornstarch and water mixture. Keep stirring as the sauce thickens, about 20 seconds. Pour the pokeweed shoots and chicken back into the serving dish and serve immediately over boiled white rice. Serves 4.

Variations: This dish is very good when ½ lb. thinly sliced beef or pork is substituted for the chicken in the marinade. Double the marinade and combine it with 1 lb. shrimp for another version.

June

*J*mperceptibly May moves on and we are into June. Our growing world is young but not too young. The multitude of wild edibles at hand now demands that we exercise a little choice. If you
did some January planning, it will come to your aid as you decide
which wild edibles to pursue first.

You may find it helpful to group your plants as to habitats;
heading for a favorite field you might have five or six foods in
mind. You probably will not locate all of them on this particular
trip, but it does produce a certain efficiency if you come home
with three or four things that you had been hoping to cook.

June's bounty is the bounty of youth. Generally speaking, if you
want a certain plant in its fairly early stage (though not necessarily
when it is a mere shoot), June is the time to look for it. Young
grape leaves to be stuffed, the buds of the milkweed, and our
early New England fruit, the strawberry—all these delicacies are
in June's larder.

A rose is a drink. You may discover, as we did, that a sip of
roseade recalls childhood dreams of a fairy princess who liked to
eat wild foods from flower cups.

We found our biggest patch of wild strawberries on land about
to be built upon. We gathered every last one, knowing we might
never again have that many for jam, sherbet, mousse and short-
cake. The berries were so thick our knees were stained red from

kneeling as we picked. Strawberries often hide under their leaves and only a shiny flash here and there gives them away. You must look closely to find all of them. Our dog gathered the small red berries alongside us. While we were unable to teach her to drop them from her mouth into our baskets, to her credit she never took a strawberry out of our collection. Our children were self-denying strawberry pickers at first. But as the afternoon wore on,

24. Beach Pea   *Lathyrus maritimus*

The beach pea is found growing along the sea coast in sand and around rocks. It has purple blossoms and tendrils like the cultivated pea. When the pods are less than an inch long and pinkish, they can be cooked and eaten whole like Chinese snow pea pods. As the beach pea plant matures the pods become quite tough, so use only the shelled peas. Pick beach peas from late June through August.

those gorgeous little fresh fruits proved too great a temptation and we had our first strawberry feast right in the middle of the patch.

Toward the end of the month the juneberries (almost julyberries) start to ripen. The children invented a way to gather them: rowing along the edge of a small freshwater pond, they collected the berries from trees hanging over the water. A quick sample and they decided they preferred them cooked. Unlike the strawberries, the juneberries all got home to the pot.

Up to now, your seaward trips have been for intertidal foraging. By June the land and air temperatures are closer to the sea's (land and air heating much faster than the sea). So you will find good foraging also in the seaside zone, above the line where the highest tides carry the salt waters but still subject to occasional splashing and dashing of saltiness. Here and now are the small, reddish pods of the beach peas, delightful additions to summer salads, soups and stews. At this very young stage, these pods are tender enough to be used in the same way as Chinese snow pea pods.

June is part of the great orchestration of summer gathering. You will have to start pacing yourself as you go through this season, choosing to swim in pond, stream or ocean when you gather edibles in these spots. Plan a forest forage on a very warm day, picnicking as well as picking. The season's joys stretch limitlessly.

STIR-FRIED BEACH PEA PODS AND BEEF

    1 lb. boneless steak, any cut
    1 tbs. soy sauce
    1 tbs. dry sherry
    1 tsp. cornstarch
    5 tbs. peanut oil
    1½ cups young, reddish beach pea pods,
        washed, ends and strings removed
    1 8-oz. can water chestnuts, drained and sliced
    1 clove garlic, minced
    1 tsp. salt
    ¼ tsp. sugar
    3 slices ginger root

Place the steak in the freezer for 1 hour. Remove it and slice as thinly as possible. Place the steak slices, soy sauce, sherry and cornstarch in a bowl, stir to coat all the slices with the marinade,

25. Catbrier, Common Greenbrier   *Smilax rotundifloria*

Catbrier is a climbing vine with hard prickers on its green stems and branches. Anyone who has ever had to clear it from land or make a path through it is familiar with its tenacious hold on life. The small yellow flowers bloom in the spring; the waxlike blue-black berries appear in the late summer and fall. The leaves are smooth and shiny and green on both sides. Pick the young, reddish catbrier shoots from dense tangles in thickets and woods from May through August.

and let it rest at room temperature for at least 30 minutes. Place a wok or heavy iron skillet over high heat for 30 seconds, add 2 tbs. peanut oil and swirl it around for 30 more seconds, coating the entire cooking surface. Add the beach pea pods, water chestnuts, garlic, salt and sugar and stir constantly for 3 minutes so that each piece is coated with oil. If the beach peas are still too crunchy for your taste, add 2 tbs. water to the pan, cover tightly and cook for 2 more minutes. Remove the vegetables to a serving dish and place the wok or skillet over high heat once again. Add the remaining 3 tbs. of peanut oil and the 3 slices of ginger root. Stir for 1 minute, remove the ginger slices and add the marinated beef. Stir constantly until every piece of beef is browned, from 3 to 5 minutes. Add the cooked beach pea pods and water chestnuts and stir for 30 seconds to thoroughly combine everything; pour into serving dish and serve immediately over white rice. Serves 4.

CATBRIER SHOOT SALAD

2 to 4 cups catbrier shoots, using only the first 3 to 6 inches of the tips
¼ cup French dressing *(see page 19)*

Boil the shoots in salted water for 2 minutes. Drain, cool and pour your French dressing over them. Serves 4.

Variations: Raw shoots are edible if you use only the tenderest part of the tips. The shoots are also a pleasant addition to any mixed green salad.

VEGETARIAN STUFFED GRAPE LEAVES

20 grape leaves
3 cups water
1½ tsp. salt

Pick grape leaves measuring about 6 inches across and trim off all stems. Bring salted water to a boil and add grape leaves. Boil 5 minutes, then rinse leaves under cold running water and make the stuffing.

Stuffing

3 large onions, chopped and sprinkled
with 1 tsp. salt to soften them

½ cup uncooked rice, rinsed in warm water
⅓ cup parsley, freshly chopped
4 fresh mint leaves, finely chopped
2 tbs. pignolia nuts (pine nuts)
2 tbs. currants
½ cup olive oil
¼ tsp. salt
4 grinds pepper
1 lemon, thinly sliced
2 cups water

Mix all the stuffing ingredients (onions, rice, parsley, mint, pignolia nuts, currants, olive oil, salt and pepper) together. Place each cooked grape leaf flat on the cutting board with the stem end facing you. Put 1 tsp. of stuffing ⅓ of the distance from the stem end and roll the bottom third of the leaf around the stuffing. Fold the right and left sides of the grape leaf over your first roll and finish rolling it away from you. It should look like a little cigar or rounded envelope. (The technique is similar to the way a butcher wraps meat.) Pack the stuffed grape leaves tightly in a heavy casserole and place the thinly sliced lemon and water on top of them. Put a heatproof plate over the grape leaves and lemon slices, cover and bake in a 350° oven for 1½ hours. Serve cold with freshly sliced lemons. Serves 10 as an hors d'oeuvre or 4 as an entrée.

STUFFED GRAPE LEAVES

60 to 70 grape leaves
4 cups water
2 tsp. salt

Pick grape leaves measuring about 6 inches across and trim off all stems. Bring salted water to a boil and add grape leaves. Boil 5 minutes, then rinse leaves under cold running water and make the stuffing.

Stuffing

1 lb. ground lamb
2 cups cooked rice
2 minced onions
½ cup chopped parsley
½ cup pignolia nuts (pine nuts)

26. Grape, Northern Fox Grape   *Vitis labrusca*

     Grapes grow on a long leafy vine climbing or trailing along the edges of woods and roads. It is difficult to distinguish among the wild species; they vary in size, color (green to purple) and sweetness of fruit, but they can all be used. Pick the young leaves in June, the unripe grapes in August and the ripe grapes in September and October.

½ tsp. chopped fresh rosemary (¼ tsp. dried)
1 tsp. salt
¼ tsp. pepper
1 to 2 cups water

Thoroughly combine all the stuffing ingredients. Put 1 tbs. of stuffing 1 inch from base of flattened grape leaf. Roll as directed in the Vegetarian Stuffed Grape Leaves recipe. Place layers of stuffed grape leaves in covered pot with 1 to 1½ cups water. (You may add chopped tomatoes, lemon or other seasoning to the water.) Cook over medium heat for 45 to 60 minutes. Taste a leaf and if it isn't tender, cook 10 to 15 minutes longer. You may prefer to bake them in a 350° oven for 1 hour. Serve as a main course with salad or as hors d'oeuvres. They may be frozen before or after cooking. Serves 8 as an hors d'oeuvre or 4 as an entrée.

JUNEBERRY JAM

4 cups juneberries, hulled and washed
3 cups sugar
4 sterilized 6-oz. jars

Place the juneberries and sugar in a saucepan. Squeeze ½ cup of the berries to make some liquid so the remaining mixture does not burn. Cook over medium heat 30 minutes. Strain and pour into the sterilized jars. (Sterilize jars by immersing them in boiling water for at least 20 minutes.) Refrigerate. Pour a layer of melted paraffin on top if you intend to keep the jam for more than a month.

Variation: Pour the mixture unstrained into the sterilized jars if you like a more textured, whole fruit jam.

JUNEBERRY SYRUP

3 cups juneberries
1 cup sugar
1 tbs. triple sec or kirsch

Simmer the hulled and washed juneberries and sugar for 20 minutes. Strain, add the liqueur and boil the syrup 1 minute. Cool and serve over ice cream, crêpes, cake or pudding.

27. Juneberry, Shadbush, Serviceberry *Amelanchier* (20 species)

Small clusters of white flowers bloom among dark-green leaves for less than 2 weeks in late May or early June. Dark clusters of juicy berries appear in late June through August, ranging in color from red to dark purple to blue-black. The shrub variety grows from 3 to 7 feet; the tree grows up to 20 feet tall. Juneberries are found in open land, the edges of woods and water, rocky areas and even along the edges of swamps.

28. Milkweed   *Asclepias syriaca*

Milkweed is common in most open areas, particularly along roads and fields. Pendulent clusters of flowers grow lavender, pink and brown in midsummer. The large gray-green leaves grow on 3- to 5-foot stalks. In late summer the green seed pods are evident. In fall, children or nature open the dried pods and release the flat brown milkweed seeds on their white silken parachutes. Pick the new shoots and flower buds in May and June, the leaves in July, and the pods in August.

MILKWEED BUDS IN YOGHURT DRESSING

    2 cups milkweed buds, washed
    1 kettleful of boiling water

Place the milkweed buds in a small saucepan, cover with boiling water and boil 2 minutes. Pour off the water and cover the buds with fresh boiling water from the kettle. Boil 2 minutes and repeat the process, boiling the buds 6 minutes for the third and final cooking. Drain and chill at least 1 hour before tossing with yoghurt salad dressing. Serves 4.

Yoghurt Salad Dressing

    1 cup yoghurt
    2 to 3 tbs. tomato sauce or ketchup
    1 tbs. chopped parsley
    1 tbs. grated fresh horseradish

Mix the ingredients thoroughly and combine with the chilled milkweed buds.

MINT VINEGAR

    1 cup cider vinegar
    ¼ cup sugar
    ½ cup mint leaves

Bring the vinegar to a boil and add the sugar and mint. Continue to boil the mixture gently for 5 minutes, crushing the mint with the back of a spoon to release as much flavor as possible. Strain the liquid through cheesecloth; squeeze the cheesecloth tightly to extract every drop of liquid possible. Keep the bottle in the refrigerator and use it to flavor fruit punches, ice tea or fresh fruit compote. You can also add honey to it and use it as a sauce for lamb.

ROSEADE

    1 cup wild-rose petals, washed
    2 cups water
    juice of 1 lemon
    ½ to 1 cup sugar

When you pick the rose petals, stack them in the same direction between your fingers and clip off the white base (remember to bring scissors or a knife when foraging). This white base is very bitter in some roses and not nearly as bitter in others so it is a good idea to nibble a few to determine whether you should clip off all the bases. Mix the petals, water, lemon and ½ cup of sugar in a blender until the drink is frothy and pink. Sample it and add more sugar if necessary. Fills 4· 6-oz. glasses.

Variation: Add ½ cup less water and use as a mixer with gin or vodka.

29. Wild Rose *Rosa* species

There are many wild species such as carolina, rugosa, setigera, eglanteria, *with branches ranging from 1 to 6 feet in height. Their stems tend to be more prickly than those of the cultivated varieties. They grow along roadsides and clearings. Pick the white or pink blossoms from June to August, and the round red or orange hips in August and September.*

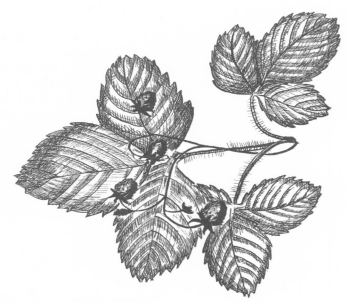

30. Strawberry *Fragaria virginiana*

Wild strawberry plants grow 3 to 6 inches high in fields and clearings. Three green, hairy, toothed leaves are attached to each leaf stalk. The white, 5-petaled flowers bloom on a separate stem in April and May. It is easy to pick strawberries clean from their hulls, when ripe in June. Don't miss any of the small, red, delectable fruits; they may be hidden underneath the leaves.

WILD STRAWBERRIES À LA RUSSE

    1 cup heavy cream
    ½ cup milk
    ½ cup sugar
    1 pinch salt
    1 envelope unflavored gelatin
    ¼ cup cold water
    ½ cup sour cream
    2 tbs. kirsch or ½ tsp. vanilla extract
    1 to 2 cups hulled wild strawberries,
           sweetened with 1 tbs. sugar if desired

Cook the cream, milk, sugar and salt in a saucepan over low heat, stirring constantly until the sugar is dissolved and the mixture almost comes to a boil, approximately 5 to 10 minutes. Soften the gelatin in ¼ cup cold water and quickly stir it into the hot cream mixture until it is dissolved. Refrigerate for 10 minutes. Use a blender, whisk or eggbeater to combine thoroughly the sour cream, liqueur and the cooled cream mixture. Pour into a heart-shaped mold and chill until firm. Unmold and serve on a plate, surrounded by berries. Serves 4.

Variations: Try different shaped molds or make 4 to 6 individual molds. Use different fresh fruit in season such as raspberries, blackberries or blueberries and try other liqueurs like triple sec, cognac or substitute ½ tsp. of lemon, orange or almond extract.

WILD STRAWBERRY JAM

1 cup freshly picked strawberries, hulled
¾ cup sugar
2 or 3 sterilized baby-food jars or small glasses

Mash ¼ cup of the berries in the bottom of a small enamel or stainless-steel saucepan to make some liquid so the mixture won't burn. Add the rest of the berries and sugar and bring to a boil, stirring occasionally for 20 minutes. Pour into the sterilized jars and cover with a layer of paraffin if you intend to keep the jam for more than a month. Attach the sterilized lids and label.

STRAWBERRY SHERBET

4 cups wild strawberries, hulled
2 cups sugar
1 cup water
½ cup lemon juice
1 cup orange juice
2 tbs. orange liqueur

Bring the sugar and water to a boil, turn the heat down and cook gently until the mixture becomes a syrup. Add the lemon and orange juices and strawberries. Pass the mixture through a sieve and add the liqueur. Pour into a mold and freeze at least 3 hours. Serve the sherbet unmolded on a plate, surrounded by fresh strawberries. Serves 4.

Variations: Use 4 cups of any fresh wild fruits in season. Blueberries, blackberries and raspberries are especially good.

July

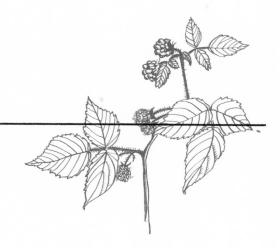

$\mathcal{T}$his month, for the wild-food forager as well as for the patriot, is a red, white and blue banner time. While we cannot find the stars in the banner, unless we count the star-shaped dried petals at the top of each shiny rose hip, July is truly a time of colors and celebration.

We are now in blueberry heaven. Locally, every serious blueberrier has his secret patch. He may brag about how big and plentiful the berries are, "they just fall into your pail," but he never gives precise directions to the spot. It does not hurt to take along mosquito repellent when you go blueberrying, in addition to a pail (tradition calls for a metal coffee can with a wire handle) or two pails if you are a fanatically dedicated picker. Picking clean, without leaves or twigs, is an admirable art. Another refinement is preferring only the true blueberries, although an occasional dark huckleberry in no detectable way detracts from the good blueberry flavor.

The first blueberries to ripen are the low-bush variety. As they are picked out, nature cooperates by offering a new source: the high-bush blueberries. Picking these requires less stooping and true New Englanders appreciate going from the harder to the easier.

Cultivating some vegetables to supplement the wildings offers

75

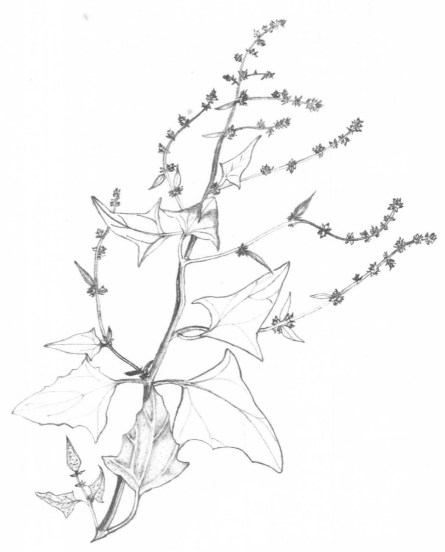

31. Orach *Atriplex halimus*

Orach grows in clumps 1 to 2½ feet high along the sea shore.
Though similar to lambsquarters its leaf is a slightly darker green with a
lighter underside; its veins are heavier and the stem and leaf are longer.
Orach is at its best in July but the younger leaves can be gathered through
September. It is easy to overlook this seaside plant despite its height, for
it has a rather nondescript look.

an unexpected dividend. The ploughed and fertilized soil of the vegetable patch will produce particularly nice volunteers of purslane and lambsquarters. Much to our neighbors' amazement, we carefully mulched around the roots of these "weeds" so that along with their tame relations they would grow big and beautiful. However, as these are hearty plants they require no pampering for survival.

July is so generous we feel a little ungrateful if we do not save some of her gifts for leaner times. The simplest way is by drying. Day lily buds, their spent flowers, and sea lettuce can be spread on trays, covered with cheesecloth if necessary, and left in an attic or furnace room until brittle. Stored in airtight containers (sealed plastic bags are good), these dried plants are welcome additions to winter soups, stews and drinks. Dig up the long tap roots of the chicory plant in late July and scrub them well. Cut in half lengthwise and roast in a 250° oven for 1 to 2 hours, or until the inner white parts of the roots are brown and brittle. Grind the roots in a coffee grinder or blender and store in an airtight container in a cool place. So natural to do, drying seems not to violate the rule of each in its own time.

A few lucky days of late July rain will bring a crop of chanterelle mushrooms. Quite by chance, we spotted some growing on a lawn at the edge of a sun-dappled wood. Finding these bright orange delicacies, which look like umbrellas turned inside out by a sharp gust of wind, was thrilling. Here were French specialities growing in our own rockbound New England back yard. You need not be a mycologist to recognize chanterelles; they are distinctive. Study the drawing and description (Figure 33) carefully, and if you are still in doubt consult a knowledgeable neighbor or any of the books on mushrooms listed in the bibliography.

SEASIDE VEGETABLES AND FISH

    2 tbs. beach peas
    4 cups orach leaves, washed
    4 tbs. peanut oil
    1 tsp. salt
    ½ tsp. sugar
    1 garlic clove, finely minced
    ¼ tsp. fresh ginger root, finely diced
    1 lb. filet of sole, haddock, cod or other firm-fleshed
        white fish, cut into 1-inch cubes

77

Boil the beach peas in ¼ cup water for 5 minutes and drain. Heat 4 tbs. peanut oil in a wok or cast-iron skillet over high heat for 30 seconds. Add the orach leaves and stir constantly until they are wilted, about 3 minutes. Add the drained beach peas, salt and sugar and stir for 1 minute. Remove mixture to serving dish. Heat the remaining 2 tbs. peanut oil in the skillet over high heat and add the garlic, ginger and fish. Stir constantly until the fish is cooked, about 3 to 5 minutes. Pour the cooked vegetables back into the skillet and stir over medium heat for 1 more minute to combine everything thoroughly. Serve over boiled rice. Serves 4.

BLUEBERRY CAKE

½ cup butter or margarine
1¼ cups sugar
2 eggs, well beaten
2½ cups all purpose flour
2½ tsp. baking powder
½ tsp. salt
½ cup milk
1 cup blueberries, hulled and washed

Cream the butter and sugar. Add the 2 beaten eggs. Sprinkle 1 tbs. of flour over the blueberries and mix so that every blueberry is lightly dusted with flour. This tends to keep the blueberries evenly distributed throughout the batter. Combine the remaining dry ingredients and sift them into the cake mixture alternately with the milk. Add the floured blueberries and mix well. Grease a 9 by 9 by 2-inch pan and pour the batter into it. Bake in a 375° oven for 35 to 45 minutes. This cake is good for breakfast, lunch or dinner dessert.

BLUEBERRY ICE CREAM

6 cups blueberries, hulled and washed
3 cups heavy cream
2 cups milk
1 tsp. lemon juice
1½ cups vanilla sugar

To make vanilla sugar bury a vanilla bean in a canister of sugar. Use this special vanilla sugar for homemade ice creams and

32. Blueberry   *Vaccinium angustifolium*

Blueberry bushes grow in acid, well-drained soil in open areas and along the edges of woods, roads and water. They also grow well in old burnt-out areas so check these places 3 years after the fire for new crops. Both the low-bush blueberry (1 to 2 feet high) and the high-bush blueberry (3 to 10 feet high) have white or pinkish flowers in the spring. After a wet spring, the berries are particularly large and numerous. You may find low-bush blueberries in late June, although most blueberries ripen in July and August. Don't overlook its frequent neighbor, the huckleberry bush, whose fruits are blackish and shiny.

sherbets. Substitute 1½ cups regular sugar and 1½ tsp. vanilla extract if you have no vanilla sugar. Blend all ingredients in a blender and strain into the container of your ice-cream maker. Never fill the container more than ¾ full. Put the dasher and cover on the container and place it in your ice-cream maker. Attach the gear case and handle. Pack 8 parts of crushed ice to 1 part of rock salt in layers to the top of the container. Crank until the mixture is half-frozen (about 15 minutes). Add 1 cup of whole berries if desired. Drain the water from the tub, repack the tub with 8 parts of crushed ice to 1 part of rock salt and continue cranking. The ice cream should be ready in 10 to 15 more minutes. Remove the lid and dasher. Cover the ice-cream container with foil and put just the lid back on with a cork in the hole. Drain the water and repack the tub with 4 parts crushed ice to 1 part rock salt. Let stand 2 hours and serve. Fourth of July is not complete without a dish of blueberry ice cream covered with juneberry sauce and sliced almonds for a red, white and blueberry dessert.

BLUEBERRY TART

> 1 baked 9-inch pie shell (or a 10- to 12-inch French quiche ring
>   for an elegant-looking tart)
> 3-oz. pkg. of cream cheese
> 1 tbs. sugar
> 1 tsp. cognac or vanilla
> 4 to 5 cups blueberries, washed and hulled
> 1 cup water
> 1 cup sugar
> ¼ cup cornstarch, completely dissolved in ¼ cup cold water
> ⅛ tsp. salt
> 1 tbs. butter
> 1 to 2 cups heavy cream
> 1 tbs. sugar
> ½ tsp. vanilla

Use a fork to combine thoroughly the cream cheese, 1 tbs. sugar, and cognac and spread it on the warm pie shell *(see page 81)*. Combine 1 cup each of blueberries, water, sugar, and the salt and the cornstarch mixture. Cook over medium heat, stirring occasionally, until the mixture thickens and turns translucent. Add the remaining 3 to 4 cups of blueberries (depending on the size of your pie crust) and pour the warm mixture into the cream-cheesed pie crust. Chill the tart for 2 to 3 hours. Whip the heavy cream until thickened. Add vanilla and 1 tbs. sugar and whip until fairly stiff. Serve each piece of the tart with a generous dollop of whipped cream. Serves 6 to 8.

Variations: Try making this tart with 4 to 5 cupfuls of raspberries, strawberries, blackberries or any other wild fruit.

PIE CRUST

(enough for a top and bottom 9-inch crust or two bottom 9-inch crusts)

1 tsp. salt
2 cups sifted flour
1 cup shortening or lard
¼ cup cold water

Sift the flour and salt into a medium-sized mixing bowl. Cut in the shortening with 2 knives or a pastry blender. Add cold water, mix and add more water, 1 tsp. at a time, if needed to make a firm, slightly moist pie dough. Divide in half and roll out one crust at a time with a floured rolling pin on a floured board or counter. The bottom crust should be 1 to 2 inches larger in diameter than the pie plate. Roll the pastry around the rolling pin and unroll it onto the pie plate. Pour in filling and cover with top crust. To partially bake a bottom pie crust before filling, prick the bottom and sides and bake in the upper third of a 425° oven for 10 minutes. Serves 6.

CHANTERELLES ON TOAST

1 cup chanterelles
2 tbs. butter
1 tbs. flour
¼ tsp. salt
4 grinds pepper
2 to 3 tbs. dry white wine
¼ cup beef bouillon
4 slices of white sourdough toast

Clean the chanterelles with a damp towel and slice. Melt butter over low heat. Stir in chanterelles and cook for 20 minutes, stirring gently every 5 minutes. Add the flour and stir over medium heat for 2 minutes. Add the salt, pepper, wine and bouillon and stir until thickened. Serve on sourdough toast for an unforgettable hors d'oeuvre. Serves 4.

Variation: If you gather more than 1 cup of chanterelles, increase the sauce accordingly and serve it over poached fish or chicken.

33. Chanterelle *Cantharellus cibarius*

Chanterelles have chrome-yellow, funnel-shaped caps; their white flesh has the delicate fragrance of apricots. The caps measure from 1 to 4 inches across and their edges are usually rolled under; the solid stems are 1 to 3 inches long. The thick, forked gills run partially down the stem and have small cross-veins connecting them. Locate small groups of chanterelles from July to September in woods and shaded lawns, particularly under pines and hemlocks. The only poisonous species with which a chanterelle could possibly be confused is the jack o' lantern (Clitocybe illudens), which is luminescent and grows in clumps. Take specimens into a dark room, close the door, and if they glow, throw them away.

STIR-FRIED DAY LILY BUDS

2 to 3 cups washed day lily buds
½ 8-oz. can water chestnuts, sliced
2 tbs. peanut oil
1 tsp. salt
¼ tsp. sugar
¼ cup water
1 tsp. cornstarch dissolved in 1 tbs. water

Heat a heavy iron skillet or wok over high heat for 30 seconds and pour in the peanut oil and swirl it around for 30 seconds. Add the day lily buds and stir constantly until all are covered with oil, approximately 1 to 2 minutes. Add water chestnuts, salt, sugar and water and stir some more. Then cover the skillet and steam for 1 to 2 minutes. Stir the cornstarch and water mixture, pour into the vegetables in the skillet, and stir everything until the sauce is thick and shiny, about 20 seconds, and remove from heat immediately. Serve at once. Serves 4. The remaining water chestnuts can be refrigerated in a covered jar filled with water. Change the water every 5 days and they will keep for 2 to 3 weeks.

34. Elderberry, Elder   *Sambucus canadensis*

Elderberry bushes grow from 4 to 10 feet high along roadsides, in moist soils and thickets. The leaves are smooth and a medium shade of green. In June and July the flowers, or elderblow, bloom in showy white clusters that are flat on top. July's flowers will become August's berries so don't pick them all. In August and September strip the deep-purple clustered berries from their purple stems.

ELDERBLOW WINE

1½ qts. stemmed elderflowers
3 gals. boiling water
2 tbs. lemon
5 lbs. sugar
1 pkg. yeast (wine yeast if available)
3 lbs. raisins

Combine the first 4 ingredients and let the mixture cool to 100°. Cooling takes at least 5 hours so gather your elderflowers early in the day. Pour 1 cup of the lukewarm mixture over the yeast to soften it. Combine the softened yeast and elderflower mixture in a crock or clean plastic garbage pail and let it stand for 9 days. Strain the mixture into gallon bottles, distribute the raisins equally and cap loosely. Store the young wine in a cool dark place for 6 months or longer. Carefully siphon or pour the wine into sterile bottles and enjoy! This is a dessert wine and is especially good over sliced fresh fruit, or in a wine punch.

LAMBSQUARTERS QUICHE

1 cup purée of lambsquarters
1 9-inch partially baked pie shell
2 cups thinly sliced potatoes
1 cup onion slices
2 tbs. butter
2 eggs
½ cup milk
½ to 1 tsp. salt
4 grinds pepper
3 tbs. Parmesan cheese

Collect at least 4 cups of lambsquarters leaves, steam them in ¼ cup of water for 5 minutes and purée in blender for 30 seconds. Boil the potatoes in 2 cups salted water for 10 minutes. Sauté the onion slices in the butter until soft and golden. Place one layer of the partially cooked potatoes on the pie crust *(see page 81)*; pour the purée on top, next the cooked sliced onions and then the remaining potatoes. Beat together the eggs, milk, salt, pepper and cheese and pour over the potatoes. Bake in a 350° oven for 30 minutes or until a knife inserted in the center comes out clean. Serves 4.

Variations: Use an orach purée and ¼ tsp. less salt. Add spinach leaves or lambsquarters leaves if you don't have enough fresh orach.

35. Lambsquarters, Pigweed *Chenopodium album*

These leafy plants grow in gardens, where they're always being weeded out, and along roads and fields. Their strong stems are 5-sided and their green leaves halberd-shaped, with light-green undersides. The older stems and leaves turn purplish-scarlet towards the end of summer, when the green seed pods form a pyramid of small cones at the top of the plant. Pick them from July to October.

POTAGE BONNE FEMME

4 cups sheep sorrel, washed and finely chopped
1 cup purslane
5 tbs. butter
2 medium onions, finely chopped
3 tbs. flour
2 cups broth (meat or vegetable) or water
2 cups milk
1 to 2 tsp. salt
1 tsp. sugar
1 tbs. chervil and/or parsley
1 egg

Add chopped lettuce or spinach leaves if you cannot find enough sorrel. Sauté the onions in butter for 5 minutes. Add the sorrel and purslane and sauté 5 more minutes. Add the flour and sauté 2 minutes; slowly add the broth and milk and bring the mixture to a boil. Add the salt, sugar, chervil and parsley and simmer for 20 minutes. Beat the egg and mix in ½ cup of the hot soup. Stir the beaten egg mixture into the soup and taste. Correct seasonings if necessary and serve. Serves 4.

Variation: Place a freshly toasted piece of French bread in each soup bowl and pour the soup over it.

36. Purslane   *Portulaca oleracea*

Purslane grows along the ground, spreading its low branches 3 to 10 inches over the soil. Its succulent green paddle-shaped leaves are attached to reddish, round stems. It grows on open land, waste places and cultivated garden soil from June to October.

RASPBERRY OR BLUEBERRY CLAFOUTIS

1 partially baked pie crust, in a 1½- to 2-inch-deep,
    9-inch diameter, pie pan or baking dish
2 to 3 cups raspberries or blueberries
3 eggs
½ cup sugar
⅓ cup flour
½ cup heavy cream
1 scant cup milk
2 tbs. kirsch or 1 tsp. vanilla

Place the berries in the pie-crust shell *(see page 81)*—no more than 2 or 3 layers deep. Beat the eggs and remaining ingredients together thoroughly. Pour the custard mixture over the berries and bake in a 375° oven for 50 to 60 minutes or until a knife stuck in the center comes out clean. Serves 4 to 6.

Variations: Place the fruit in the bottom of a buttered baking dish. Cover with the above custard mixture and bake according to directions. Lightly sprinkle confectioners' sugar over the clafoutis when it comes out of the oven. Also try making it with other fresh fruit or berries in season.

ROSE PETAL JELLY

2 cups fresh wild-rose petals
1½ cups boiling water
1 cup honey
2 tbs. lemon juice
2 apples, grated

Cover the rose petals with boiling water and let steep for 30 minutes. Strain the liquid into a heavy enamel or stainless-steel pan and add the honey, lemon juice and grated apples. Bring the mixture to a boil and continue boiling gently for 20 to 30 minutes, stirring regularly. After 20 minutes check the mixture with this jelly test. Dip a metal spoon into the liquid and see if 2 drops form and then run together as they cool. If not, continue cooking and testing every 5 minutes. When your mixture passes the jelly test pour it into sterilized jars and seal with paraffin if you don't intend to use it right away. After a jar of jelly has been opened, keep it in the refrigerator.

37. Raspberry   *Rubus* species

Raspberry bushes grow 2 to 6 feet high on well-drained clearings and dry slopes. The leaves are green on top, whitish underneath, and are attached to rather woody, prickly stems. Its white flowers in spring become ripe red berries in July and August.

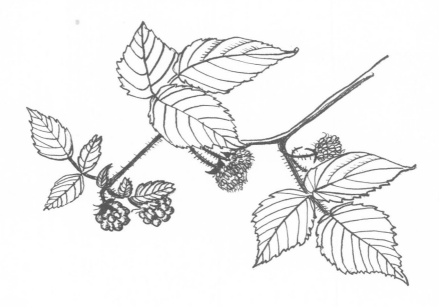

ROSE SUGAR COOKIES

   ¼ cup wild-rose petals
   3 tbs. boiling water
   1 tsp. lemon juice
   2 tsp. sugar
   ½ lb. butter
   2 cups sugar
   1 egg
   4 tbs. rose elixir
   2 tbs. medium cream
   4 cups flour

Blend the first 4 ingredients until the petals are thoroughly liquefied. Cream the butter and add 2 cups sugar, egg, rose elixir and cream. Sift the flour into the mixture 1 cup at a time until a

38. Chicory, Blue Sailor *Cichorium intybus*

   The light-blue chicory flowers bloom sporadically during the day from July to September. The dark-green ragged leaves look like those of an awkward, overgrown dandelion. Chicory grows in very poor soils along fields and roads, varying from 1 to 4 feet in height. Pick the young tender greens for salad from late March to July; dig the roots for coffee in July and August.

thick dough is formed. Roll the dough into 2 or 3 cylinders (approximately 2 inches in diameter), wrap in wax paper and chill in the refrigerator for at least 1 hour; you may freeze some of the dough at this point for later use. Preheat oven to 400°. Cut the refrigerated dough into rounds ¼ inch thick and place them on lightly greased cookie sheets at least 1 inch apart. Press a fresh rose petal into the center of each cookie and bake 8 to 10 minutes. Cool on racks and store in a dry, airtight container where they will keep for 1 to 2 weeks.

Variations: Use commercial rose water instead of rose elixir. Use only 1 tbs. and increase the cream by 3 tbs. Garnish with sliced almonds, aniseeds or coriander seeds.

SEA LETTUCE SALAD

> ½ cup fresh sea lettuce
> 1 clove garlic
> 1 cup fresh chicory leaves, washed and torn into bite-size
>   pieces
> 2 cups lettuce, washed and torn into bite-size pieces
> 1 tsp. minced chives
> ¼ cup radishes, thinly sliced
> 1 tbs. wine vinegar
> 3 tbs. olive oil
> ½ tsp. salt
> 4 grinds pepper

Rinse sea lettuce in 2 changes of fresh water and cut into thin strips. Rub salad bowl with garlic and fill with salad greens. Pour 1 tbs. of olive oil over the greens and toss well. Then add the vinegar, salt, pepper and remaining oil and toss until each leaf is coated with dressing. Serves 4.

Variations: Add ¼ tsp. dry mustard dissolved in the vinegar, 1 tsp. chervil or basil, or 1 cup watercress.

August

*T*he notes of summer swell as July passes into August. Indeed, the comparison with a great symphony is not too far-fetched. Rachel Carson found "contemplation of the motion and beauty of form of living nature yields aesthetic enjoyment of as high an order as music or painting."

August is rooted in the realities of hot sun, dusty plants beside back country roads, ponds that have lost the bracing quality of one's first plunge. Growth is carried irresistibly along to its goal of fruition and maturity. August has weight and seriousness; she is firmly set in her course.

Set aside the early hours of the day for picking. The sun still rises very early and it is a joy to be out with the first freshness of the day. We try to cook our jams, custards, soups and stuffed milkweed pods before the great buzz of an August day has reached its hot pitch, or late in the day, as the sounds fold in on themselves and the sun casts longer shadows. The midday sun works for us, drying red clover blossoms spread on trays set out in a protected corner while we take it easy.

We sadly pick the last of the blueberries. We resolutely pick the first blackberries, in jeans and long-sleeved old shirts to help breach the blackberries' immense tangle of briar. But blackberries are worth the effort, including our fall into an unseen hole in the midst of a briar patch where we beheld an enormous spider who seemed to be chuckling, as though he had planned our drop.

Birds like elderberries as much as we do. We often race with them for the choicest bushes. They pluck a berry at a time, the way we do so that we will know just how many cups we have picked. Our children pick whole clusters of elderberries and hull them later in the shade, seated on cool granite steps.

The staghorn sumac is easy to identify. (Only the poison sumac has dangling clusters of whitish berries; its leaves are shorter and fatter than those of the staghorn.) Sumacade, pink and partylike, is the perfect drink for children to sell at their summer sidewalk stands. This delicious drink attracts more customers than do the powdered, synthetic, storebought concoctions.

One hit and one miss in August foraging has taught us to keep a substitute ingredient on the menu, just in case the day's expedition does not bring in the hoped-for wild edible. A nearby cemetery had supplied us with fresh puffballs (if their centers are powdery or even yellow, they are not fresh enough to eat) every two to four days after a rain. With a burst of confidence, we invested in a turkey, intending to stuff it with a batch of these mushrooms. However, no rain, no puffballs, no stuffing, or so we thought. But unripe grapes inspired us to concoct a green-grape stuffing and jelly to serve alongside and we saved our turkey investment.

BLACKBERRY BAVARIAN

    2 cups washed blackberries
    1½ cups sugar
    ¼ cup water
    2 envelopes unflavored gelatin
    ¼ cup cold milk
    2 eggs
    1½ cups sour cream
    1 cup crushed ice

Cook the blackberries, sugar and water over medium heat for 20 minutes. Strain the syrup through 2 layers of cheesecloth to remove the seeds. Sprinkle the gelatin over the milk to soften it. Bring the strained blackberry syrup to a boil and pour it over the softened gelatin, stirring to dissolve the granules. Pour the gelatin mixture and all the remaining ingredients into a blender and whirl for 30 seconds until everything is thoroughly combined. Pour the mixture into an oiled 5-cup mold or bowl. Chill at least 2 hours and unmold onto a serving dish. (Dip the mold in hot water for 10 seconds and run a sharp knife around the edge of the Bavarian. Place a serving plate over the mold and invert it onto the plate.) Surround the Bavarian with fresh blackberries and blueberries. Serves 4 to 6.

39. Blackberry *Rubus allegheniensis*

The leaves of a blackberry bush are bright green; the stems are hairy and covered with prickers. The black, juicy oblong fruits are easily freed from their hulls when ripe. The bushes grow 3 to 7 feet high in clearings and along roadsides. Pick the young shoots for salads in April and May; pick the fruits in August and September.

BLACKBERRY JULEP

2 cups washed blackberries
1 cup sugar
¼ cup water
6 sprigs fresh mint gently bruised (optional)
1 quart club soda
1 lemon, thinly sliced

Cook the blackberries, sugar and water over medium heat for 20 minutes. Strain the syrup through 2 layers of cheesecloth into a container. Add the mint sprigs, cover container and refrigerate for at least 6 hours. Pour 2 oz. of julep into a glass, add ice cubes and 4 to 6 oz. of soda. Garnish with a slice of lemon. This syrup will keep in the refrigerator for months, and can be frozen in ice-cube trays for individual servings up to a year.

Variations: Add a jigger of vodka or gin for a new summer highball. You may also substitute any fresh berry in season such as raspberries, strawberries or blueberries.

BLUEBERRY GINGERBREAD

½ cup margarine or butter
1 cup sugar
1 egg or 2 egg yolks
2 cups all purpose flour
½ tsp. ginger
1 tsp. cinnamon
½ tsp. salt
1 cup sour milk or buttermilk
    (or add ¼ cup sour cream to ¾ cup milk, mix thoroughly
    and leave at room temperature for at least 10 minutes)
1 tsp. baking soda
3 tbs. molasses
1 cup wild blueberries mixed with 1 tbs. flour
3 tbs. sugar

Cream the margarine or butter and 1 cup sugar. Add the egg (2 egg yolks make a richer cake) and mix well. Sift together the flour, ginger, cinnamon and salt. Dissolve the baking soda in the sour milk and add to the creamed mixture alternately with the sifted dry ingredients. Stir in the molasses and the floured blueberries.

Pour the batter into a greased and floured 9 by 9 by 2-inch pan. Sprinkle the 3 tbs. sugar evenly on top of the batter and bake in a 350° oven for 50 to 60 minutes. This cake is delicious warm, cool or even 2 days old if you can keep it around that long.

BLUEBERRY SOURDOUGH PANCAKES

1½ cups starter *(see p. 22)*
2 cups water
2½ cups flour
1 egg
2 tbs. oil
¼ cup dry or evaporated milk
1 tsp. salt
1 tsp. baking soda
2 tbs. sugar
1 cup wild blueberries

The night before, mix up the starter, water and flour in a 2-quart nonmetal bowl leaving the batter somewhat lumpy. Let it sit at room temperature overnight. The next morning put 1½ cups of the batter into your starter jar and add the egg, oil and milk to the remaining batter. Combine salt, baking soda and sugar separately and sprinkle over the batter. Fold in gently and watch the batter go into action. It should become 2 to 4 times bigger in less than 5 minutes. Drop 1 tbs. of batter on a hot, lightly greased griddle for each pancake. Sprinkle some blueberries over each uncooked pancake and when the top becomes dull turn it over. Or you can mix blueberries into the batter, but stir each time before dropping batter onto the griddle to make certain the fruit is distributed evenly. If this batter seems too thick, add a little more milk, but always make pancakes silver-dollar-sized. Serves 4.

Variations: Substitute wild strawberries, raspberries, rose petals, grated apples or mashed bananas for blueberries; or omit the sugar and add finely chopped clams, mussels or periwinkles for a luncheon dish.

BRAVO BOLETES

1 cup boletes
2 tbs. butter
salt and pepper to taste

Wipe the tops of the boletes with a damp towel and peel off the skin if it is very sticky. Cut them into ¼-inch slices and throw away any specimens that have bug tunnels. Melt butter in a small saucepan over medium heat; add the boletes and sauté for 2 to 3 minutes. Season with a little salt and pepper and serve immediately. Serves 4 as an hors d'oeuvre or 2 as a vegetable.

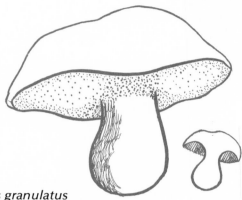

40. Boletes   *Boletus granulatus*

The caps of boletes look like sticky brown or reddish-brown buns, with undersides a mass of tiny pores rather than gills. Their fleshy stalks are 2 to 6 inches long, ½ to 1½ inches thick, with somewhat bulbous ends. They grow around the bases of pine trees and in birch woods from July through September. To test for edible boletes, look at the tips of the pores or tube masses; if they are red or pink, throw the specimen away. Next, bruise the pores on the underside with your finger; if they turn blue, throw the mushroom away. Then cut each one in half and look for bug tunnels; if there are none and the firm flesh is white or yellowish, eat and enjoy it.

CHOKECHERRY BRANDY

5 cups washed chokecherries
2 cups water
3 cups sugar, approximately
1 pint brandy (low or medium priced,
     depending on your taste and pocketbook)

Cook the chokecherries and water over medium heat in an enamel or stainless-steel pan for 30 minutes. Place a 20-inch square of unbleached muslin or a double layer of cheesecloth in a sieve or colander. Pour the stewed chokecherries on top and let

41. Chokecherry   *Prunus virginiana*

The leaves of the chokecherry are dark green and smooth with fine serrations along the edges. The chokecherry is more a high shrub than a tree, growing 5 to 25 feet tall along roads, streams and in thickets. The pea-size cherries grow in dark red clusters ripening to black in August, when they should be picked. Eat a raw cherry to find whether you really do choke over its somewhat astringent taste.

the juice drip through. This will take a couple of hours. Squeeze the cloth around the pulp to extract all the liquid possible. Measure the chokecherry juice and add twice that amount of sugar. Cook the syrup for 5 minutes and strain into a measuring pitcher. For every 2 cups of syrup add 1 cup of brandy and pour into sterilized wine bottles and cap. Sample it when cool. At this point a tasting party may be necessary to determine if these proportions are agreeable to you and your friends. If not, add more chokecherry juice or brandy until you arrive at your own special blend. Make note of your proportions so you can duplicate your own blend of chokecherry brandy next summer.

Variations: This brandy is excellent served on ice as an apéritif, or mixed with soda water and ice for a cooling end-of-summer highball.

CHOKECHERRY JELLY

> 5 cups washed chokecherries
> 1 cup water
> 3 cups sugar, approximately
> ½ bottle pectin

Cook the chokecherries and water over medium heat in an enamel or stainless-steel pan for 30 minutes. Place a 20-inch square of unbleached muslin or a double layer of cheesecloth in a sieve or colander. Pour the stewed chokecherries on top and let the juice drip through. This will take a couple of hours. Squeeze the cloth around the pulp to extract all the liquid possible. Measure the chokecherry juice and add twice that amount of sugar. Bring the syrup to a boil, stirring constantly. Add the pectin and boil rapidly while stirring for 1 minute. Skim off any foam on top and pour the syrup immediately into sterilized jars or glasses. Cover with paraffin or canning tops and store in a cool cupboard.

Variations: If you prefer a natural pectin, cook 4 chopped apples (including peels and cores) in 1 cup of water for 30 minutes. Strain the juice through muslin or cheesecloth and measure it. Combine equal amounts of apple and chokecherry juice. Measure the combined syrup and add an equal amount of sugar. Boil gently, stirring constantly for 10 minutes or until the syrup passes the jelly test *(see Rose Petal Jelly recipe, page 87)*. Pour into sterilized jars and cover.

STUFFED DAY LILY BLOSSOMS

12 to 16 day lily blossoms,
    rinsed in cold water, with stamens removed
3-oz. pkg. cream cheese
1 tsp. milk
⅓ cup Monterey Jack or cheddar cheese, grated
1 tsp. salt
4 grinds pepper
1½ tbs. canned minced green chili peppers
¼ cup flour
½ cup vegetable oil
2 eggs
1 tsp. water

Mix the cream cheese and milk with a fork. Add the grated cheese, salt, pepper and minced chilis. Place approximately 1 tsp. of filling in each blossom and pinch or twist the tips together. Roll each stuffed blossom in flour and refrigerate for at least 1 hour before cooking. Heat ¼ inch of vegetable oil in a skillet over medium-high heat. Beat the 2 eggs with 1 tsp. water and dip each floured blossom into the mixture. Fry the blossoms until golden brown on each side, drain on paper towels and serve on a plate garnished with freshly picked day lilies. Serves 4.

ELDERBERRY JAM

4 cups of just ripened elderberries,
    stripped from stems and washed
2 cups apples, cored and chopped with their skins
    (use wild apples if available)
½ tsp. salt
½ cup orange juice
2 to 4 cups sugar

Put the elderberries, apples, salt and orange juice in an enamel or stainless-steel saucepan, bring to a boil and simmer uncovered 20 to 30 minutes. Mash the cooked fruit through a colander or coarse strainer. Measure the purée and add 1½ cups of sugar to each cup of purée. Return the sweetened purée to the saucepan and cook over low heat, stirring constantly for 15 to 20 minutes. Pour the jam into sterilized jars or glasses and cover with paraffin if you don't intend to use all the jam within a month. This jam is especially good in omelets or crêpes.

MUSHROOM SALAD

½ cup field mushrooms,
    cleaned with a damp towel and sliced
½ cup French dressing *(see page 19)*
¼ cup purslane leaves, washed
¼ cup watercress, washed
1 tbs. glasswort, diced
3 cups Boston lettuce,
    washed and torn into bite-size pieces
1 tbs. parsley
1 tsp. fresh basil, minced

Marinate the sliced field mushrooms in French dressing while you prepare the rest of the salad ingredients. (The longer they

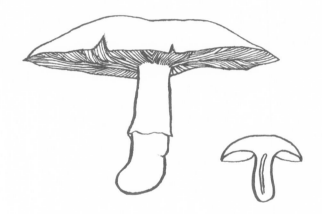

42. Field Mushrooms   *Agaricus campestris*

The caps of field mushrooms grow 1 to 5 inches across; they are smooth and white but turn brown with age. The gills, not attached to the stem, are a light, delicate pink but also turn brown with age. There can be a ring near the middle of the 2- to 3-inch-long stem, but it may be missing on older specimens. The flesh is firm and white and stays white when bruised. Dig up the entire specimen to see whether the base is cup-shaped; if it is, throw the mushroom away. Field mushrooms are related to the cultivated mushrooms sold commercially. During long periods of moist, cool weather from August through October, look for field mushrooms in fields, lawns, and rich manured ground, but never in woods.

marinate, the better they are. A tightly covered jar of mushrooms and French dressing keeps for at least a week in the refrigerator.) Combine the remaining ingredients in a salad bowl. Pour the mushrooms and dressing over the salad ingredients; toss and serve immediately. Serves 4.

GOLDENROD TEA

5 to 6 fresh, fully open goldenrod flowers
4 cups boiling water
Sugar or honey to taste

Strip the fresh goldenrod flowers from their stems and place in the bottom of a warm teapot. You should have at least 4 to 5 teaspoons of flowers. Cover them with boiling water and steep for 10 minutes. Sweeten the tea with a little sugar or honey. Dry goldenrod flowers on a tray in the sun or attic for use year round. If any of your guests happen to be allergic to goldenrod serve them mint tea. Serves 4.

UNRIPE GRAPE MINT JELLY

3 cups washed unripe grapes
⅓ cup water
1 cup sugar, approximately
½ cup washed fresh mint leaves
1 tsp. Madeira (optional)

Cook the grapes and water for 10 minutes or until the skins are popped. Let the cooked pulp drip through 2 layers of cheesecloth for 3 hours. Squeeze out the remaining liquid and measure it. You should have about 1 cup. Measure an equal amount of sugar into a pie plate and warm in a 300° oven for 10 minutes. Meanwhile combine the unsweetened grape juice and mint leaves in an enamel or stainless-steel saucepan and boil gently for 10 minutes. Remove mint leaves with a slotted spoon, add the warm sugar and Madeira and cook 5 minutes or until the mixture passes the jelly test *(see page 87)*. Pour into sterilized jars and cover with a layer of paraffin. This jelly is excellent with turkey, ham, lamb or roast beef; it is also an important ingredient in October's Grape Tart.

43. Goldenrod   *Solidago odora*

Goldenrod consists of graceful feathery rods covered with delicate eight-petaled golden flowers and slender leaves which exhibit translucent veins when held up to light. When crushed, the leaves give off a subtle anise scent. Goldenrod grows 1 to 3 feet high along roads, in dry open woods and poor soils, and blooms from July to September.

UNRIPE GRAPE STUFFING FOR TURKEY

    1 10-lb. turkey
    6 to 8 grape leaves, stemmed and washed
    ½ cup butter or margarine
    1 turkey liver, finely chopped
    2 onions, diced
    1 cup bread crumbs
    4 cups cooked rice
    1 cup unripe grapes, halved and seeded
    ¼ cup pignolia nuts (pine nuts) or sliced almonds
    2 eggs
    1 tsp. salt
    10 grinds pepper
    1 tsp. chervil
    1 tsp. sugar

Melt the butter or margarine and sauté the turkey liver and onions in it for 5 minutes. Add the liver and onions to the remaining stuffing ingredients and spoon into the lightly salted turkey cavity. Close the opening with skewers and rub the skin of the turkey with 2 tbs. of butter or margarine. Cover the greased turkey with the grape leaves and bake in a 350° oven for 3 hours, basting with pan juices every 20 minutes. Remove the grape leaves, turn the oven to 400° and roast the turkey for 20 more minutes. Place it on a serving platter to cool while you make the sauce.

Sauce

    4 tbs. drippings from the roasting pan
    4 tbs. flour
    2 tbs. Madeira
    2 cups chicken stock
    ½ tsp. salt
    10 grinds pepper

Place the drippings in a saucepan over low heat. Stir in the flour for 1 minute. Add the Madeira, stock, salt and pepper and beat with a whisk until the sauce thickens. Pour into a serving bowl. Serves 8 to 10.

STUFFED MILKWEED PODS WITH SAUCE

20 to 24 milkweed pods,
    about 2 to 3 inches long
    (press them between your fingers
    and pick only the firm ones)
1 kettleful of boiling water
1 cup bread crumbs or bread stuffing mix
¼ cup onion and celery, finely diced and mixed
¼ cup diced puffballs
    or any other available edible mushrooms
3 tbs. butter or margarine
2 tbs. water or chicken broth
1 egg, beaten
¼ tsp. salt
3 grinds pepper

Wash the milkweed pods and place in a small saucepan. Cover them with boiling water from the kettle, add ¼ tsp. salt and boil for 5 minutes. Drain them and repeat the process twice, boiling the pods for only 1 minute the final time. Drain and let them cool while you sauté the onions, celery and puffballs in 3 tbs. butter for 5 minutes. Add them to the bread crumbs and mix in the remaining ingredients. Slice each milkweed pod along its seam and remove the cooked down, which you can add to the stuffing if you like. Fill each pod with 1 to 2 tsp. of stuffing and place them in an oven-proof baking dish.

Sauce

2 tbs. butter or margarine
2 tbs. flour
¾ cup milk
¼ tsp. salt
3 grinds pepper
1 dash of freshly grated nutmeg
⅓ cup grated Swiss or Parmesan cheese

Melt the butter, stir in the flour for 1 minute and add the milk, salt, pepper and nutmeg, stirring over low heat until thickened. Add the grated cheese and when it melts, pour the sauce over the stuffed milkweed pods and bake them in a 350° oven for 15 minutes or until nicely browned. Serves 4.

Variation: Try this same recipe with young milkweed leaves in July and August; just wrap them around the stuffing like crêpes or cannelloni.

CANDIED MINT LEAVES

> 100 well-formed mint leaves
> 1 egg white
> 1 to 2 cups superfine granulated sugar
>   in a shaker or fine sieve

Clean and dry the leaves thoroughly. Beat the egg white until it is almost stiff and brush a fine film on both sides of each leaf. Sprinkle the sugar evenly on both sides of each leaf, or dip leaves into a plate of sugar. Lay the leaves on waxed paper and dry in the refrigerator or a cool place. Store in an airtight container between layers of wax paper and use as cake decorations or individual candies.

STUFFED MUSSELS

> 1 qt. mussels, cleaned and debearded
> 1½ cups boiling water

Prepare the Vegetarian Grape Leaf Stuffing given in June's recipes *(see page 65)*. Steam the mussels in 1½ cups of boiling water for 5 minutes or until they are opened. Strain the broth and save for later. Remove and discard the top mussel shells. Place a teaspoonful of the stuffing on the bottom mussel shell, completely covering the attached mussel. Place the stuffed mussel shells in the bottom of a large casserole with a tight-fitting cover. Gently pour the strained mussel broth around the stuffed shells. If you do not have 2 cups of broth, add water. Cover the casserole and cook it in a 350° oven for 1 hour. Serve warm with fresh lemon wedges. Serves 4.

ORACH PASTA

> ½ cup orach purée
> 4½ cups flour
> ½ tsp. salt
> 2 eggs beaten

Allow at least 2 hours to prepare this recipe the first time you try it. Collect 4 cups orach (or substitute lambsquarters if you happen to be inland), cook 5 minutes in ½ cup water and purée at your blender's highest speed. Place 2 layers of cheesecloth in a sieve and pour purée on top. Squeeze hard to remove all excess water. Put the flour and salt in a bowl, make a depression in the center and pour in the eggs and purée. Mix with your hands until the dough forms a rough ball. Turn the dough on a counter or table top and knead 5 minutes. Add more flour, 2 tbs. at a time, until the dough is extremely stiff. Divide the dough into 4 equal parts and roll into long thin sheets no more than 6 inches wide. Set the dial of your pasta machine at the widest opening and run the dough through. Run the dough through 3 more times, decreasing the setting 2 or 3 notches each time. Attach the noodle cutter and run the dough through it. Drape the pasta over the backs of your kitchen chairs and let dry at least 30 minutes. If no pasta machine is available, roll the dough as thin as possible, cut into ½-inch wide strips and let dry at least 30 minutes. Cook the pasta in a large pot of boiling water for 8 to 10 minutes. (Fresh pasta cooks faster than fully dried pasta.) Drain and toss with 2 tbs. butter. Serve with Periwinkle and Beach Pea Spaghetti Sauce or plain tomato sauce. Serves 4 to 6.

PERIWINKLE AND BEACH PEA SPAGHETTI SAUCE

½ cup cooked periwinkles
    (collect at least 2 cups of periwinkles)
2 tbs. beach peas
    (collect at least 1 cup of beach pea pods)
2 tbs. olive oil
4 medium cloves garlic, finely chopped
1 tbs. flour
¾ cup clam juice, mussel juice or fish stock
¼ cup white wine
1 tbs. parsley, finely chopped
1 tbs. grated Romano or Parmesan cheese
    (substitute grated Sap Sago for a unique taste)
¼ tsp. salt
3 grinds pepper

44. Periwinkle *Littorina litorea*

The common periwinkle has a drab-gray or black, slightly conical shell, ½ to 1 inch in diameter. A periwinkle feeds on algae and can live out of water for a while if it closes its operculum. The tide does not have to be very low in order to pick periwinkles from the rocks in any season.

Rinse the 2 cups of periwinkles in fresh water and boil in 1 cup of water 5 minutes. Cool and unscrew the meat from the shells with toothpicks or small metal skewers. This may take ½ to 1 hour. Be sure to discard the flat little brown disc that covers the mouth of the shell and may still be attached to the meat. Sauté the garlic and beach peas in olive oil for 2 minutes over moderate heat. Add the flour and continue stirring for 1 minute. Add clam juice, wine, parsley, cheese, salt and pepper and simmer gently 5 to 10 minutes. Add the periwinkles, cook 2 more minutes, taste, correct seasonings, and serve over orach pasta or plain spaghetti. Serves 4 to 6.

Variations: Substitute clams or mussels for periwinkles, small garden peas for beach peas.

PUFFBALL FRITTERS

1 cup of puffballs
¼ cup flour
½ tsp. salt
4 grinds pepper
1 tsp. finely chopped parsley and chervil
1 egg
1 tsp. milk
3 tbs. butter

Wipe the puffballs with a damp cloth and cut off the base if soil clings to it. Peel the skin if it is tough; slice. Mix the flour, salt, pepper and herbs in a small bowl. Dust the puffball slices with the flour mixture. Beat together the egg and milk in another bowl and dip the floured puffball slices in it. Melt the butter in a skillet over medium heat and fry puffballs until golden brown, no more than 10 minutes. Serves 4.

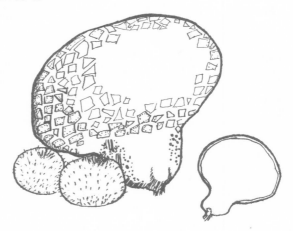

45. Puffball   Genus *Calvatia* and *Lycoperdon*

Puffballs are round or pear-shaped fungi, whose spherical tops taper to a narrow, stemless base. Their exterior colors range from white to brown and they measure 1 to 4 inches across; they have no gills and exhibit a smooth homogenous interior when cut in half. All species are edible if their insides are firm and white, but always use them immediately. Discard all specimens with brownish interiors. Old puffballs belch gray or black smoky powder when punctured; don't inhale as this dark powder may irritate your trachea. Puffballs grow in open meadows and hardwood forests from July through October.

PUFFBALL SURPRISE

1 cup of puffballs, chopped
2 tbs. butter
¼ tsp. salt
2 grinds pepper
4 pieces bacon, cooked and crumbled into small pieces
    (or substitute 2 tbs. grated Swiss or Parmesan cheese)
½ cup cottage cheese
½ cup margarine
1½ cups flour

Mix the cottage cheese, margarine and flour together to make a smooth pastry. Refrigerate for 10 minutes. Wipe the puffballs with a damp cloth and cut off the base if soil clings to it. Tough skins should be peeled. Chop puffballs and sauté in the butter, adding the salt, pepper and bacon or cheese. Dust a counter top or cutting board and your hands with flour and press 1 heaping tsp. of dough into a circle. (Use a rolling pin if the dough is firm enough.) Put 1 tsp. of the puffball mixture in the middle of the circle and top with a second circle of dough. Seal the edges with a fork. Place the filled and sealed pastries on an ungreased baking sheet and bake in a 350° oven for 20 minutes or until golden. Serves 4.

PURSLANE DIP

1 cup chopped purslane
1 pint sour cream
3 scallions, finely chopped, and/or 1 tsp. minced onion
1 small container of red caviar
salt, pepper or Tabasco (optional seasonings)

Combine all the ingredients and place in a serving bowl. Refrigerate for 1 hour. Serve with chips or crackers. Serves 4 to 6. (This dip will lose its crunchiness if prepared too many hours in advance or kept overnight.)

ROSE HIP JAM

2 cups diced rose hips,
    their stems, flower ends and seeds removed

2 cups sugar
1 cup water
2 apples, peeled, cored and diced
   (use wild apples if available)
4 tbs. lemon juice

Bring the sugar and water to a boil in an enamel or stainless-steel saucepan and boil gently for 4 minutes to form a thin syrup. Add the apples, rose hips and lemon juice. When the mixture begins to boil again, cover and boil gently for 15 minutes, stirring occasionally. Strain the mixture through a colander or coarse strainer and return it to the saucepan. Cook gently for 3 to 4 minutes, stirring constantly. Pour into sterilized jars and seal tightly. Cover the jam with ¼-inch layer of paraffin if you intend to keep it longer than 1 month.

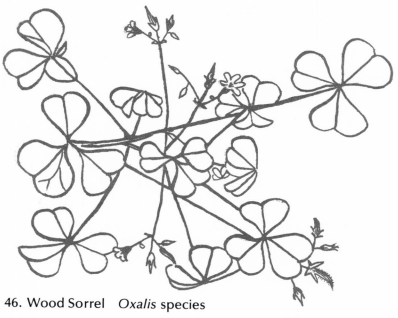

46. Wood Sorrel   *Oxalis* species

The bright-green clover-shaped leaves of wood sorrel have 3 petals. The small, 5-petaled flowers can be yellow, white or pink. Wood sorrel has a milder, less lemony taste than sheep sorrel. The 6- to 16-inch-high plant thrives in poor, rocky soil, and along the edges of lawns and woods from April to October.

SORREL SOUP À LA GRECQUE

    2 cups wood sorrel
    2 tbs. butter
    4 cups chicken broth
    ½ cup uncooked rice
    2 eggs
    ½ tsp. salt
    1 tsp. sugar
    4 grinds pepper

Sauté sorrel in the butter for 2 minutes. Add ½ cup of the chicken broth to the cooked sorrel and whirl in a blender for 10 seconds. Bring the remaining 3½ cups of chicken broth to a boil and add the rice. Cover and cook over medium heat for 20 minutes. Beat eggs until frothy, combine with the sorrel mixture and add 1 cup of the hot chicken and rice soup. Stir the egg, sorrel and soup mixture into the rest of the hot soup and add the salt, pepper and sugar. Cook over medium heat, stirring constantly, for 3 minutes. Do not stop stirring or overheat this soup or the eggs will scramble. Serve immediately. Serves 4.

SUMACADE

    2 cups sumac berries
    1 qt. water
    sugar to taste

Bruise and mash the sumac berries in the water until water turns a rich pink. Strain the drink carefully through several layers of cheesecloth to remove the sumac bristles and stalks. Sweeten to taste with sugar, refrigerate, then serve. Serves 6 to 8.

TANSY CUSTARD

    4 eggs
    ½ cup sugar
    1½ cups medium cream
    1 tbs. cognac
    ¼ tsp. freshly grated nutmeg
    ½ cup walnuts, finely ground
    ½ tsp. fresh tansy flowers, pulverized in a mortar
        (or use ¼ tsp. of dried tansy flowers)
    2 tbs. citron, finely chopped, tossed with 1 tsp. flour

Beat the eggs thoroughly; add the sugar, cream, cognac and nutmeg and beat for 2 minutes. Stir in the walnuts, tansy and floured citron and pour into a 5- to 6-cup baking or soufflé dish. Place in a bain-marie (pour boiling water into a larger pan and place the filled baking dish in it). Bake in 325° oven for 60 minutes. If a sharp knife inserted into the center of the custard comes out clean, the custard is cooked. If liquid adheres to the knife's surface bake the custard 10 minutes more. Test and remove from the oven when cooked. Cool at least ½ hour before serving. Serves 4.

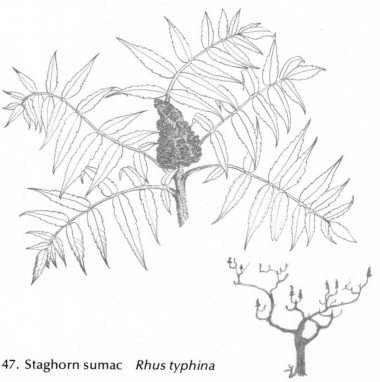

47. Staghorn sumac   *Rhus typhina*

The newer branches of staghorn sumac are covered with velvet fuzz. The leaves are dark green in the summer, turning to brilliant reds and oranges in the fall. Staghorn sumac grows in dry soil, along roads and clearings; its height varies from a shrub size of 4 to 6 feet to a maximum tree size of 20 feet. Break off the dark-red cones of berries from late July through October. Choose only those that are fresh as the older ones may harbor insects. Avoid the poisonous variety of sumac, which has white fruit.

48. Tansy, Bitterbuttons *Tanacetum vulgare*

The leaves of the tansy plant are strongly scented and are shaped like a feather fern; try them in salads in May when they are young. The flat clusters of bright-yellow tansy flowers look somewhat like daisies (in the same family) without petals. Tansy grows from 1 to 4 feet high along roadsides and in open areas; gather the flowers from July to September.

September

*P*aradoxically, September is both a continuation of August as well as a season of change, often a clear-cut change that can occur immediately after Labor Day. To those on the seacoast, a northeast storm may bring the first new smells of the season. Inland, a tropical hurricane may dramatically strip green leaves and create premature gauntness.

While August is dark green and dusty, September is golden and misty. Mushrooms react with a burst to September's moisture and coolness. The mushrooms of September which we include all have very distinctive features. There are no look-alikes to confuse the uninitiated. Rather than try to cover the entire subject, we suggest six sure bets that will enable you now to have the fun of using wild mushrooms. (Refer to the pictures and descriptions given for morels, field mushrooms, sulfur shelf mushrooms, chanterelles, puffballs and boletes.) Further study will expand your range of identification should you care to go deeper into the subject. Sliced mushrooms dry well on trays in the sun and keep in airtight containers in cool cupboards. They may be revived by pouring a little hot water over them in a nonmetal bowl and letting them sit for 30 minutes.

Jerusalem artichokes release August's sun in September flowers. You can dig the tuberous roots early in the month

114

although they are tastier after a touch of frost. Note where the flowering plants are at the beginning of September and gather during the first cold snap of the month.

We know a dramatic heath, too hot in summer, too bleak in winter, but perfect in September. It is now awash in smokey asters, goldenrod and the running flames of the blueberries' leaves. We go there for juniper berries. Among the glacial debris of rough granite boulders, the dark-green and spicy common junipers provide lively contrast, as do their close relatives, the so-called red cedars. These plants seem to have been selected with careful consideration as to how they would look together.

Long afternoon walks beside the ocean are particularly peaceful and rewarding now that summer visitors are gone. This is the time to spot the glasswort with its tips touched red by autumn. Orach is often a close seaside neighbor and may also have bright red tips now. We reluctantly head home with the last few inches of our baskets crammed with mussels. September tempts us to linger by the sea.

FIELD MUSHROOMS AND ANCHOVIES

        4 cups field mushrooms,
            cleaned with a damp cloth and sliced
        2 tbs. olive oil
        2 tbs. butter
        2 cloves garlic, minced
        3 whole anchovies, finely chopped
        1 tbs. lemon juice
        2 tbs. parsley, minced

Melt the butter in the olive oil in a skillet over medium heat. Add the garlic and mushrooms and stir constantly until the mushrooms are tender, about 5 minutes. Add the anchovies and lemon juice and stir for 1 minute. Sprinkle parsley on top and serve immediately. Serves 4.

Variations: Remember that some people don't like anchovies. You can either omit the anchovies from this recipe or remove a portion of the cooked mushrooms before adding the anchovies and serve according to your guests' preference.

FIELD MUSHROOMS IN SOUR CREAM

1 lb. mushrooms,
    cleaned with a damp towel and sliced
3 tbs. butter
1 tbs. flour
½ tsp. salt
2 grinds pepper
1 cup sour cream
2 tsp. grated Parmesan cheese
2 tbs. chopped parsley or 2 tsp. chopped dill

Sauté the mushrooms in the butter for 3 to 5 minutes, add the flour, salt and pepper and stir for 1 minute. Blend in the sour cream and pour the mixture into a shallow heatproof platter or baking dish. Sprinkle with grated cheese and brown under a broiler for 1 to 2 minutes. Garnish with the chopped parsley or dill and serve. Serves 4.

MUSHROOM LOAF
WITH TARRAGON CREAM SAUCE

1 lb. mushrooms (4 to 5 cups of field mushrooms),
    cleaned, trimmed and finely minced
3 scallions, minced
3 tbs. butter
2 tbs. flour
½ cup milk
3 eggs
½ cup cream
½ cup bread crumbs
½ cup finely minced cooked chicken or ham
    (or substitute ¾ cup grated Swiss cheese)
1½ tsp. tarragon
½ tsp. salt
4 grinds pepper
pinch of nutmeg, freshly grated

Sauté the mushrooms and scallions in the butter for 5 minutes, add the flour and stir for 1 minute. Pour in the milk and stir over low heat until thickened. Beat the eggs and add the cream, bread crumbs, chicken, tarragon, salt, pepper and nutmeg. Combine with the mushroom mixture and pour into a 1- to 1½-qt. casserole or soufflé dish that has been lightly buttered and dusted with bread crumbs. Place in a bain-marie (pour boiling water into a larger pan and place the filled baking dish in it) and cook in a 375° oven for 25 minutes or until a knife stuck in the center comes out clean. Serve the loaf in its dish or unmold it and coat with the following sauce.

Tarragon Cream Sauce

    ½ cup heavy cream
    ½ cup milk
    2 tsp. tarragon
    ¼ tsp. salt
    2 grinds pepper
    2 tbs. butter
    1 tbs. flour

Combine the cream, milk, tarragon, salt and pepper in a small saucepan and bring to a boil. Simmer for 10 minutes. Mash the butter and flour together with a fork (to make a beurre manié) and stir into the hot sauce until it thickens. Spoon over each serving of mushroom loaf. Serves 4.

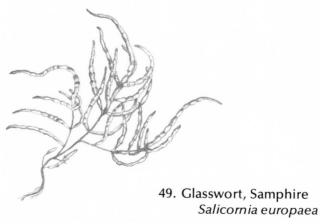

49. Glasswort, Samphire
Salicornia europaea

Glasswort grows from 2 to 10 inches tall in saltmarshes and on clay shores that get wet only during high tide. The spikes are attached to a tough stem; they are a light translucent green from May to September, before they start turning red. They can be eaten through November.

GLASSWORT AND
JERUSALEM ARTICHOKE SALAD

1 lb. cooked Jerusalem artichokes, peeled and diced
1 cup glasswort
½ cup Italian, French *(see page 19)* or cress dressing *(see page 126)*

Remove the roots and the brownish parts of the glasswort stems and cut the rest into ½-inch pieces. Combine the above ingredients in a bowl and toss with dressing before serving. Serves 4.

GRAPE PIE

5 cups wild grapes, washed and stemmed
1⅓ cups sugar
4 tbs. flour
1 tsp. lemon juice
1 pinch salt
1 tbs. butter

Remove the skins from the grapes by pressing the bottom of the grape, which allows the grape to pop through the hole in the skin where the stem was removed. Save the grape skins for later. Put the pulp in a saucepan and bring to a rolling boil. Force the hot pulp through a food mill or strainer to remove the seeds. Add the grape skins, sugar, flour, lemon juice and salt to the strained pulp and pour it into a bottom pie crust *(see page 81)*. Dot with small lumps of butter and cover with a top crust. Prick the top crust in a few places with a fork or knife. Bake in a 425° oven for 35 to 45 minutes. The top crust should be nicely browned and the grape juices should be bubbling through the slits. Serves 6 to 8.

JUNIPER RATAFIA

3 tbs. juniper berries
⅛ tsp. cinnamon
¼ tsp. coriander
4 pinches mace
1 pt. brandy
½ cup sugar
½ cup water

Put the juniper berries, cinnamon, coriander and mace in a mortar and bruise the berries and spices together gently with a pestle. Add the mixture to the brandy and let steep for 2 weeks. Strain the mixture and discard the berries and any sediment. Put ½ cup sugar and ½ cup water in a small saucepan, bring to a boil and simmer for 10 minutes over medium heat. Pour the sugar syrup into the juniper brandy and sample when cool. This is a pleasant drink before or after dinner. It can also be added to a fresh fruit compote. Serves 10 to 12.

50. Juniper *Juniperus communis*

The evergreen juniper usually grows from 3 to 10 feet tall but it can reach almost 20 feet. The ultrasharp ½-inch-long needles have green undersides and gray tops with a thin white line down the center. They grow in groups of three around the central stalk. Junipers are found in dry rocky soils on hills and pastures; the berries are about ¼ inch in diameter. Pick the ripe bluish-black berries from late August through October and leave the unripe gray berries for the birds. Juniper is quite aromatic.

JUNIPER AND MUSHROOM SAUCE FOR
ROAST CHICKEN, DUCK OR TWO GAME HENS

2 cups of your own or storebought bread-crumb stuffing
    (add the diced bird's liver and 1 minced onion
    sautéed in 1 tbs. butter)
4 to 6 slices thin bacon
5 juniper berries
4 tbs. drippings from roasting pan
1 cup sliced mushrooms
    (field mushrooms or puffballs are best)
2 tbs. flour
¼ tsp. thyme
½ tsp. salt
6 grinds pepper
¼ cup white wine
1 cup cream

Stuff the bird, cover its breast and legs with the bacon, place the juniper berries around it in a roasting pan and bake in a 350° oven 20 to 25 minutes per pound. Cool the cooked bird on a serving platter for 20 minutes before carving. Place 4 tbs. drippings and the juniper berries from the roasting pan in a skillet and sauté the mushrooms in it for 5 minutes over low heat. Remove the juniper berries. Sprinkle the flour over the mushrooms and stir for 1 minute. Add the seasonings and white wine and cook for 2 minutes. Then add the cream and stir until thickened. Taste and correct seasonings if necessary. Serves 4.

MOULES MARINIÈRE

2 cloves garlic
1 medium onion, chopped
¼ cup parsley, chopped
1 stalk celery, chopped
2 tbs. olive oil
1½ cups white wine
½ tsp. salt
4 grinds pepper
2 to 3 qts. mussels

Scrub the mussels thoroughly and debeard them. Sauté the first four ingredients in the hot oil, add the wine, salt and pepper and bring to a boil. Add the mussels, cover and steam until the shells open (usually 5 to 10 minutes). Serve in bowls with the broth and lots of French or Italian bread for dipping. Serves 4.

ORACH SOUP

6 to 8 cups orach leaves, washed
2 tbs. butter
1 small onion, minced
2 tbs. flour
4 cups hot chicken broth

Steam the orach for 10 minutes and season to taste with salt, pepper and a little butter. Melt 2 tbs. butter in a 2-qt. saucepan. Add the onion and sauté until golden. Stir in the flour and add the hot chicken broth, stirring constantly until slightly thickened. Pour 1 cup of the hot broth and the cooked orach into the blender and purée. Combine the puréed mixture with the remaining hot broth, heat 2 to 3 minutes and serve. Serves 4 to 6.

Variations: Use only 3 cups broth and stir in 1 cup light cream after combining the cooked orach with the hot broth. Top either soup with a spoonful of sour cream sprinkled with chives over each serving.

ORACH AND KIELBASY CASSEROLE

6 cups orach leaves, washed
½ cup water
1 lb. kielbasy sausage
¼ tsp. freshly grated nutmeg
¼ cup beer
¼ cup light cream or milk
2 tbs. flour
¼ tsp. powdered mustard
3 drops Tabasco sauce
¼ tsp. Worcestershire sauce
¼ tsp. salt
4 grinds pepper
2 cups grated cheddar cheese

Place the orach and water in a saucepan, bring to a boil, cover and cook over medium heat for 7 minutes. Drain off the excess water and stir in the nutmeg. Place the kielbasy in a saucepan, cover it with water, bring to a boil and cook for 3 minutes over medium heat. Remove the cooked sausage from the water and cut it into ¼-inch-thick slices. Combine the beer, cream, flour, cheese and remaining seasonings in a saucepan and heat gently until thickened, stirring occasionally. Spread half of the cooked orach on the bottom of a shallow buttered 1½-qt. casserole. Cover with all the kielbasy slices and top with the remaining orach. Pour the sauce over the casserole and bake in a 350° oven for 10 to 15 minutes. Serves 4.

Variations: Substitute lambsquarters and/or spinach for the orach and increase salt by ¼ tsp. You also can omit the beer and use ½ cup light cream or milk, or use ½ cup beer and no cream or milk.

WOOD SORREL GREEN SAUCE

¼ cup wood sorrel, finely minced
½ cup parsley, finely minced
½ cup chicken stock, fish stock or water
¼ cup butter
2 tbs. flour
½ cup cream
½ tsp. salt
3 grinds pepper

Melt the butter over low heat and stir in the flour. Cook for 1 minute. Add the stock, cream, salt and pepper and stir until sauce thickens. Mix in the finely minced greens, taste and correct the seasonings. The sauce should be a lovely shade of green; it goes especially well with fish, poultry or pasta. Serves 4.

Variation: 2 tbs. finely minced chives or scallions may be included.

WOOD SORREL OMELET FOR ONE

2 eggs
¼ tsp. salt
2 grinds pepper
¾ tbs. butter
1 tbs. wood sorrel, finely chopped

Beat the eggs, salt and pepper until frothy. Heat an omelet pan over medium high heat for 30 seconds; add the butter and when it melts and coats the pan pour in the eggs. Stir the eggs, being careful not to disturb the cooked bottom layer. Spread the minced sorrel over the top before the omelet sets. Tilt the pan as the eggs begin to set and lift and roll the omelet towards the opposite side of the pan. The inside will be less cooked, so the sorrel will remain almost raw. The entire process should take no more than 2 minutes. The omelet must be served and eaten at once. Never use an omelet pan for anything but omelets. Make a 2-egg omelet each time. Clean the hot pan with a dry paper towel or rag. Never use soap.

SULFUR SHELF CASSEROLE

4 cups sulfur shelf mushrooms,
    washed and thinly sliced
1 cup bread crumbs
½ cup butter
½ cup sherry
3 cloves garlic, minced
½ cup onions, chopped
½ cup green pepper, chopped
½ cup celery, chopped
1 leek, chopped
1 tsp. salt, approximately
10 grinds pepper, approximately

Use only the brightest colored, soft breakable layers of the sulfur shelf mushrooms. Throw away the tough, stringy base. Wipe the remaining brackets with a damp cloth. You may soak them in lightly salted water for 5 minutes to force out any hidden insects. Combine the chopped onions, green pepper, celery and leek in a bowl and mix them thoroughly. Butter a 1½-qt. casserole and place ⅓ of the chopped vegetable mixture in it. Place ⅓ of the sliced mushrooms over the chopped vegetables and sprinkle with salt and pepper. Then sprinkle ⅓ cup of the bread crumbs on top of the seasoned mushrooms and repeat these layers in the same order 2 more times, ending with the bread crumbs. Melt the butter in a small saucepan, add the garlic and sherry and cook over medium heat for 3 minutes. Pour the hot liquids evenly over the casserole and bake in a 350° oven for 30 minutes. Serves 4.

Variations: This casserole can also be made with 4 cups of any combination of sulfur shelf and other edible mushrooms. If the leek is unavailable, substitute 2 scallions.

51. Sulfur Shelf   *Polyporus sulphurens*

These yellow-orange, sometimes striated brackets that change to a yellowish tan when old are usually found on the trunks or bases of dead or old trees, often oaks. Their undersides are creamy white to sulfur-colored, and are covered with hundreds of minute pores. The individual brackets are from 1 to 6 inches across; sometimes they are directly attached to a tree, but usually they are fused at their bases. Gather the sulfur shelf from August through September when it's young and feels velvety; don't bother with it when it grows older and becomes chalky textured.

CREAMED SULFUR SHELF MUSHROOMS

   2 cups diced sulfur shelf mushrooms
   4 tbs. butter or margarine

1 tbs. flour
¼ tsp. mustard
½ tsp. salt
4 grinds pepper
¼ cup white wine
½ cup medium cream

One sulfur shelf mushroom usually contains 1 to 2 lbs. of edible flesh, so you can freeze the excess as is. You could also sauté the unused portions in butter and place in a freezer container; or dry ¼-inch-thick slices of sulfur shelf on trays in the sun or attic for at least 1 week and grate to a powder for use in soups, stews and gravies.

Sauté the sulfur shelf mushrooms in the melted butter over low heat for 20 minutes. Sprinkle with flour and stir for 1 minute. Add the mustard, salt, pepper, wine and cream and whisk over low heat until thoroughly blended. These creamed sulfur shelf mushrooms go well with an omelet and green salad. Serves 4.

MARINATED AND BROILED SULFUR SHELF MUSHROOMS WITH FLANK STEAK

1½ lb. flank steak
2 cups sulfur shelf mushrooms
    (sliced ¼ inch thick by 2 to 3 inches long)
⅓ cup soy sauce
2 tbs. salad oil
1 tbs. brown sugar
1 tsp. ground ginger
1 large clove garlic, finely chopped
½ cup red wine

Combine the marinade ingredients (soy sauce, oil, sugar, ginger, garlic and wine) in a covered jar and shake thoroughly. Place the steak and mushrooms in a baking dish or platter and pour the marinade over them. Marinate at least 6 hours at room temperature, turning the steak every hour or so, or marinate at least 10 hours in the refrigerator. Broil the steak and mushrooms on a rack about 4 inches from the heat source. Allow 4 minutes per side for rare steak, 6 minutes for medium and 8 for well-done. Broil the mushrooms 3 to 4 minutes on each side, and eat them by themselves if you're a vegetarian. Serves 4.

MULLED SUMAC

4 cups sumacade *(see August's recipe, page 111)*
4 whole cloves
1 stick of cinnamon
½ tsp. allspice
⅓ cup brown sugar
1 lemon
freshly grated nutmeg

Put the sumacade in a saucepan and add the cloves, cinnamon, allspice and sugar. Add thin slices of peel and juice of the lemon and heat the mixture over low heat for 20 minutes. Do not let it boil. Pour it into punch glasses or cups and add a little grated nutmeg on top. Serves 4 to 6.

Variation: Place ½ jigger of rum in each glass, then pour in the mulled sumac for a great autumnal warmer-upper.

SUNCHOKE SALAD WITH CRESS DRESSING

1 lb. Jerusalem artichokes

Scrub the sunchokes (Jerusalem artichokes) to remove all dirt. Cook in 2 to 3 cups boiling salted (½ tsp.) water for 10 to 15 minutes. Save the broth for soup *(see October's recipe, page 135)* and peel the sunchokes. Cut them into cubes and mix with cress dressing.

Cress Dressing

⅓ cup finely chopped watercress
1 hardboiled egg, sieved or finely chopped
½ cup ketchup (optional)
salt and pepper to taste
2 cups French dressing *(see page 19)*

Combine all the dressing ingredients and toss with the cubed sunchokes. Serves 4.

Variations: This dressing is also good on orach, lambsquarters, glasswort, spinach, mushrooms or alfalfa sprout salad.

52. Jerusalem Artichoke, Sunchoke   *Helianthus tuberosus*

Look for golden sunflowers 2½ inches across with yellow centers on hairy and leathery stems in September to find where to dig Jerusalem artichoke tubers. The plants grow from 4 to 10 feet tall in the damp soils of thickets and fields. Dig Jerusalem artichokes in September and October; be sure to leave some tubers for next year's crop. Jerusalem is a corruption of the Italian word for sunflower, girasole, given to the plant when it was carried back to Europe by early explorers in North America. It is in no way related to the cultivated artichoke.

October

$\mathcal{O}$ctober telegraphs one of the strongest and clearest signals of all the months of the year. Even those who live in cities start thinking about country tweeds and suedes, upland game birds and flaming leaves; they have some sense of the state of nature as they are pulled by the tide of the seasons.

For us, October is dry stone walls with bright orange and gold bittersweet berries twining among the rocks. It is the stubble of corn fields with the shocks silhouetted against the breathtaking sugar maples which line the edge of the field.

For everyone, October is pumpkins and harvest moon, Indian corn hanging on the front door, yellow chrysanthemums and . . . Here we pause and shiver slightly. For October gives us the first signals of the death of the year, of all souls, of the skeletons of trees as well as of departed people. Though we are scarcely willing to admit it, we warm ourselves as eagerly at October's leafy flames as one would warm oneself at a glorious pyre. October's message is summed up in the naming of the bittersweet.

One day last year, knowing that our mushrooming days were numbered, we went early in the afternoon to a pasture which had produced quantities of field mushrooms for us in the past. For the first time that fall we found none. But we kept walking toward the slanting sunlight, squinting and looking, hoping we would not have to go home empty-handed. We came to a little stream and saw quantities of watercress, still beautifully green and edible. Into our baskets went some cress and on we walked.

Beyond the next field lay a cranberry bog that was not boggy in an unpleasant way. We had to look carefully for cranberries, for deer and smaller wild animals like them too. We stooped down, picked up the thin trailing branches here and there, and discovered the glowing, deep red cranberries beneath the tiny leaves. The berries were attached by what looked like springing wires, almost too thin to bear their weight. We picked the large berries quickly, and headed home with a gallon of cranberries, not too disappointed about the nonexistent mushrooms.

October calls for hearty food for the forager and other out-of-doors people. It is a time for apples, sauerkraut, game, soups, sauces, and condiments for roasts. Glasswort was used by the colonists for pickles. Despite our greater range of choices for pickling, glasswort pickles are one of our favorites. October is a

53. Wild Apples
Malus species

Apple trees grow best in sunny well-drained soil. Their bark is brown and scarred from individual bud scales; their twigs are short and hairy and covered with thorny sharp buds. Their egg-shaped, toothed green leaves grow 1 to 4 inches long with white or gray, woolly undersides. Apple trees are covered with white 5-petaled flowers from late April until early June. Pick their familiar red fruits from September to November.

ter's month. Our wilding recipes will complement your
¿." Do not forget to store baskets of black walnuts and hick-
nuts in the shed, to dry out for November cracking parties.

WILD APPLE CHUTNEY

1 small onion, chopped
3 cloves garlic, chopped
1 lb. wild apples, peeled, cored and diced
1 cup cider vinegar
1 cup dates, stoned and chopped
1 cup raisins
1 cup brown sugar
2 tbs. candied ginger, minced
1½ tsp. salt
¼ tsp. cayenne pepper

Place the vinegar, onion, garlic, and apples in a saucepan, bring
them to a boil and simmer over medium heat until tender, about
20 to 30 minutes. Add the remaining ingredients and simmer 10
more minutes. Pour into 2 sterilized pint jars and seal.

CRANBERRY COCKTAIL

1 qt. cranberries
2 qts. boiling water
2 cups sugar
5 mint leaves
5 sprigs of lemon balm
        (or substitute 1 lemon peel)

Boil the cranberries, water and sugar until the berries are soft.
Rub through a sieve, add the mint and lemon balm and simmer 5
minutes. Remove the mint and lemon balm and bottle the juice.
Serve with sprigs of fresh mint, and lace it with a little vodka if
you're in the mood. Serves 10 to 12.

WILD CRANBERRY SAUCE

2 cups wild cranberries, washed
¾ cup water
1½ cups sugar

juice and grated rind of 1 orange
1 grated apple

Combine all the above ingredients in a saucepan and bring them to a boil. Let the mixture boil gently for 10 minutes or until all the cranberry skins have popped. Ladle the mixture into 3 sterilized 1-cup glass jars. Refrigerate and sample it the next day.

GLASSWORT PICKLES

4 cups glasswort
3 cups white vinegar
1 cup cider vinegar
2 to 3 tbs. mixed pickling spices
1 onion, sliced
½ cup sugar or honey
6 bay laurel leaves

Remove the glasswort's bright green and red spikes from the inedible stems and wash them. You may have to discard some of the deeper-red parts of the spikes which may be tough with age. Place the glasswort in 4 sterile 8-oz. jars. (Old baby food jars are the perfect size.) Bring the vinegars, onion, pickling spices, sugar and bay leaves to a boil and cook for 10 minutes. Pour the hot

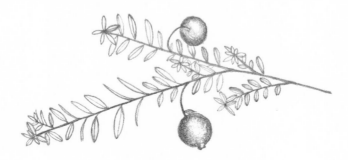

54. Cranberry *Vaccinum macrocarpon*

Cranberries grow in low-lying, wet areas that are bogs, not swamps or marshes. The pale-pink flower blooms in the spring; the small, shiny dark-green leaves persist year round. The dark-red fruit grows on hairlike brown stems which at first glance seem too thin to support the fruit. Pick the berries in September and October before heavy frosts cause them to spoil.

mixture into the jars until the glasswort is completely covered. Seal tightly and store in a cool place for at least 2 weeks before sampling. These pickles are particularly beautiful if made in September or October when the glasswort is a mixture of red and green translucent spikes. Earlier in the year glasswort is entirely green and just as good to eat pickled or fresh in a mixed green salad.

Variations: Use any proportion of white to cider vinegar. Add ½ tsp. dried mustard to the recipe for very hot pickles that are great with curries, meats or in rice salad.

GRAPE TART WITH
UNRIPE GRAPE MINT JELLY

> 5 cups washed and stemmed grapes
> ⅔ cup water
> ⅔ cup sugar
> 1 tbs. cornstarch
> 2 tbs. water
> ⅓ cup unripe grape mint jelly
> > *(see recipe for August, page 101)*

Remove the skins from the grapes by pressing the bottom of the grape. This allows the grape to pop through the hole in the skin where the stem was removed. Reserve the grape skins. Place the pulp in a saucepan with ⅓ cup water. Cook over medium heat for 5 minutes, then force the pulp through a food mill or strainer to remove the seeds. Place the strained pulp, reserved grape skins, ⅔ cup sugar and ⅓ cup water in a heavy saucepan or the top of a double boiler; cover and cook over very low heat for 1 hour. Turn the heat to medium and stir in the unripe grape mint jelly; when the jelly has melted, add 1 tbs. cornstarch completely dissolved in 2 tbs. water and stir the grape mixture until it thickens. Pour the filling into the cooked tart crust and let it cool at least 1 hour before serving.

Tart Crust

> ½ cup pulverized walnuts
> > (use a blender or meat grinder)
> 1 cup flour

½ cup butter or margarine
½ tsp. baking soda
½ cup brown sugar

Make the tart crust while the pulp mixture is slowly cooking. Mix the nuts, flour, butter, soda and sugar with a fork until crumbly. Press the mixture firmly into a 9- or 10-inch pie plate so that the entire surface is covered with crust, and bake in a 350° oven for 10 to 12 minutes or until it is nicely browned. Let the crust cool at least 20 minutes before adding the filling. A dollop of lightly sweetened whipped cream or custard sauce goes very nicely on top of a piece of this grape tart.

HICKORY OR HAZEL NUT COOKIES

1 cup hickory or hazel nut meats,
     finely ground in a nut grinder or blender
½ cup butter
3 tbs. sugar
1 tsp. vanilla
1 cup cake flour, sifted

55. Hickory Nut   *Carya ovata*

No wonder that this unkempt tree is sometimes called shagbark, for its bark splits and curls away from the main trunk. The compound leaves grow from 8 to 20 inches long, clustering in groups of five. The tree grows from 30 to 90 feet high in woods and backyards. The tan nut has a 4-valved husk and a thin white shell. Gather the nuts from September through November.

Cream the butter and add the sugar and vanilla. Alternately add the ground nut meats and sifted flour to the creamed mixture. Roll the dough into small spheres ¾ to 1 inch in diameter. Place them on a greased cookie sheet and bake in a 300° oven for 25 to 30 minutes. Delicious served with wintergreen or birch tea.

Variations: Roll the hot cookies in confectioners' sugar and cool, or return to the oven for 2 minutes to melt the sugar into a glaze. Try substituting 1 cup of black walnuts or any other wild nut you may gather.

56. Horseradish
Radicula armoracia or *Armoracia rusticana*

Horseradish grows in moist, well-drained open ground and ditches; the mature green leaves are 20 to 30 inches long in the summer. In the spring the plant has small white flowers, and the leaves are quite good in salads when they are shorter than 10 inches. Dig the white-fleshed pungent roots from April to December.

WILD HORSERADISH SAUCE

> 3 tbs. grated horseradish root
> 6 tbs. applesauce
> 9 tbs. sour cream

Blend the cleaned root in a blender with ½ cup water if the pieces are too small to grate. Strain the mixture through 2 layers of cheesecloth to remove excess water. Make wild applesauce if the fruit is handy: cover the apples with water and cook over low heat until they are soft; blend or strain and add sugar and a little lemon juice to taste. If the sauce is too thin, cook until it gets thicker. Stir the three ingredients together until thoroughly blended and chill. This sauce is especially good served with a pork loin. Serves 6.

BRAISED JERUSALEM ARTICHOKES

2 cups Jerusalem artichokes,
    washed, peeled, and cut into ½-inch cubes
1 small onion, diced
1 clove garlic, minced
2 tbs. butter or margarine
¼ tsp. bouquet garni or your own assortment of herbs
1 tsp. salt
4 grinds pepper
3 dashes freshly grated nutmeg
2 tbs. flour
¼ cup white wine
½ cup water or chicken broth

Sauté the onions and garlic in the butter for 3 minutes. Add the Jerusalem artichokes and seasonings, cover, and simmer for 20 to 30 minutes, stirring occasionally. Sprinkle the flour over the artichokes and stir for at least 1 minute. Add the wine and water and stir until the sauce is thickened. Serve garnished with freshly chopped parsley. Serves 4.

JERUSALEM ARTICHOKE SOUP

1 lb. Jerusalem artichokes, scrubbed
4 cups boiling water
1 tsp. salt
3 tbs. butter
2 tbs. mushrooms, finely diced
1 tbs. onions, finely diced
2 tbs. flour
1 chicken broth cube
1 tsp. chopped parsley
1 cup sour cream

Cook the Jerusalem artichokes in the boiling salted water for 10 to 15 minutes. Strain through cheesecloth to remove any possible dirt. Peel and dice the Jerusalem artichokes. Add ½ cup to the strained broth and use the remaining chokes for salad. Melt the butter and sauté the mushrooms and onions for 5 minutes. Add the flour and stir for 1 minute. Stir the mushroom mixture into the hot broth until it is slightly thickened. Dissolve the chicken broth cube in the hot soup and beat in the parsley and sour cream. Correct seasonings and serve in soup bowls, garnished with a slice of Jerusalem artichoke on top. Serves 4 to 6.

SAUERKRAUT WITH JUNIPER BERRIES AND WILD CARROT SEED

    1 16-oz. can sauerkraut
    1 small onion, stuck with 3 whole cloves
    6 juniper berries
    2 carrots, grated (garden variety)
    1 tsp. salt
    6 grinds pepper
    ¼ tsp. wild carrot (Queen Anne's Lace) seed
    ½ cup dry white wine
    ½ cup water

On a windy day, gather seed clusters from dried-up Queen Anne's Lace and rub them between your fingers. The wind will blow the chaff away and the cleaned seeds will fall from your fingers onto a plate. Repeat if necessary. If too much chaff still remains on the seeds, rub them in a very fine sieve. The chaff will fall through and the cleaned seeds will remain in the sieve. Store the seeds in airtight containers for use year round. Rinse the sauerkraut in cold water for 1 minute. Place all the ingredients in a saucepan and bring them to a boil. Turn the heat to low, cover and simmer gently for 1½ hours. Remove the 6 juniper berries and the cloved onion and throw away the berries and cloves. Slice the onion and return it to the sauerkraut. Serve this dish with warm kielbasy sausage and pumpernickel bread. Serves 4.

JUNIPER MARINADE
FOR WILD GAME OR BEEF

¼ cup red wine vinegar
1½ cups red wine (a burgundy is recommended)
4 juniper berries
1 bay laurel leaf
6 whole peppercorns
1 medium onion, sliced
1 small clove garlic, crushed
1 tsp. salt
4 pinches mace
2 whole cloves
⅛ tsp. thyme
4 lbs. meat or game

Combine all the ingredients and store in a covered pint jar in the refrigerator for at least a day before using. Place the meat or game in a bowl and pour the marinade over it. Turn the meat or game every couple of hours to allow the marinade to penetrate. Marinate at room temperature for 1 to 2 days depending on how strong a marinade flavor you want. Strain the marinade and use it to baste the meat or game every 20 minutes while it roasts. One pint of marinade is adequate for 4 lbs. of meat or game. Serves 8.

CREAMED PUFFBALLS

2 cups puffballs, cleaned with a damp towel
    and sliced ⅛-inch thick
1 scallion, minced
3 tbs. butter
1½ tbs. flour
2 tbs. dry white wine or vermouth
1 cup cream
½ tsp. salt
5 grinds pepper
dash of freshly grated nutmeg

Sauté the puffballs and scallions in melted butter for 5 minutes over low heat. Sprinkle the flour over the mushroom mixture and stir for 1 more minute. Slowly add the wine and cream and continue stirring until thickened. Season with salt, pepper and nutmeg; taste, correct seasonings and serve immediately. Serves 4.

November

A lucky year is one in which the first killing frost does not come until the middle of November. Unfortunately, autumn's growing days do not often last this long. But whatever the luck, one morning we will awaken to a blackened tangle of old marigold and chrysanthemum stalks. Killing frost combines with the frequent heavy rains; it is still too early for the delights of new-fallen snow. November is capable of bringing on an acute case of melancholia.

Human ingenuity has found a way of dealing with November: conscious thankfulness for the richness of the passing year and its harvest combined with the heart-warming time when friends and relatives gather together to celebrate. While October, the harvest month, might seem the more logical time to celebrate, the simple truth is that the Thanksgiving holiday is needed much more in November than in October.

Our families like to have nutcracking parties in November, because getting the nut meats out of their shells is hard work for just one person. The process has two stages: husking and cracking.

First we bring in the black walnuts from the shed where they were stored in October. (We wear rubber gloves for protection against the walnuts' dark brown stain, which can take weeks to remove.) After husking off the outer covering, we return the nuts to the shed, or other well ventilated storage spot, for a week or two to dry out. Now we are ready for the second stage: cracking.

We find conventional wooden or metal nutcrackers useless on black walnuts. So we take hammers to pound open the shells on our stone steps. The meat can be removed with ordinary nutpicks. If the weather is bad, we hold our cracking party inside on our stone hearth. To help the work go easily, we refresh our workers with hot draughts of red clover tea. Although hickory nuts are much easier to shell, the black walnuts are well worth the extra effort. They have a subtle and flavorful oil all their own, and are quite unlike the English walnuts grown commercially and found in stores.

Many of the recipes for this month provide the main elements for our Thanksgiving feast; there are some new tastes and new combinations of ingredients that fit nicely into the traditional dinner menu. We find a special reason to be thankful as we look back on almost a whole year of foraging, of learning, of feeling and of fine eating.

SWEET AND SOUR BLACK WALNUT SAUCE

¾ cup pitted dried prunes
½ cup water
⅓ cup raisins
½ cup chopped black walnuts
¼ cup butter
2½ tbs. freshly grated horseradish root
3 tbs. white vinegar
1 bay laurel leaf
½ tsp. salt
6 peppercorns
2 tbs. sugar

Stew the prunes in ½ cup water over medium heat for 20 minutes or until they are soft. Whirl the cooked prunes and their water in the blender to make a purée. Combine all the ingredients in a saucepan and cook over medium heat for 15 minutes, stirring occasionally. The sauce can be served hot or cold and will keep in the refrigerator in a covered jar for months. It is particularly good with cold ham, tongue or chicken. Makes 24 servings.

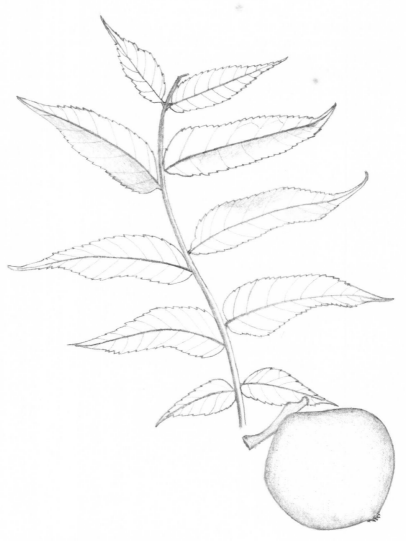

57. Black Walnut *Juglans nigra*

*Although it is more common to find black walnut trees growing 100
feet high, they can grow up to 150 feet, given room and lots of sunlight.
They are found along roadsides and clearings in rich soil; note their dark
bark and sparse leaves, which turn yellow early in the fall. A greenish
husk 2 to 3 inches in diameter tightly covers the black walnut. Gather the
nuts from September to November.*

CHICORY ROOT COFFEE

See July *(page 142)* for directions on gathering and storing chicory roots. Make a 6-cup pot of coffee and substitute ½ tsp. chicory for 1 tbs. ground coffee. Experiment with the proportions. Some people prefer greater amounts of chicory than others. Reduce the amount of regular coffee by 1 tbs. for every ¼ tsp. chicory added. Chicory coffee is also very good served with a whole bruised cardamom seed in each cup. (One coffee measure equals 2 tbs.)

CLOVER TEA

5 tsp. dried red or white clover blossoms
    (picked and dried from May to September)
4 cups boiling water
Sugar or honey to taste
Lemon slices
Mint, fresh or dried

Place the clover blossoms in a teapot and pour the boiling water over them. Let the blossoms steep 10 minutes and strain into the tea cups. Serve with sugar or honey, lemon slices and a piece of fresh mint in each cup. If no fresh mint is available, place ½ tsp. dried mint in the teapot with the clover blossoms. Serves 4.

CRANBERRY CAKE

½ cup margarine
1 cup sugar
2 eggs
1 tsp. baking powder
1 tsp. baking soda
½ tsp. salt
2 cups flour
1 cup sour cream
1 tsp. vanilla
½ cup chopped walnuts
2 cups wild cranberry sauce
    (see October's recipe, page 130)

Cream the margarine and gradually add the sugar. Blend 1 egg at a time into the creamed mixture. Combine the dry ingredients and sift ¼ of them into the creamed mixture alternately with ¼ of the sour cream. Repeat 3 more times until everything is blended and stir in the vanilla. Combine the nuts and cranberry sauce. (Melt the sauce over a low flame if it is too firm.) Butter and flour a tube pan. Pour in ½ of the cake batter and spread ½ of the sauce mixture over it; pour in the rest of the batter and then the rest of the sauce, which becomes the bottom layer of the cake after unmolding. Bake the cake in a 350° oven for 55 minutes. Cool the cake in its pan for 10 minutes before turning it over and unmolding it onto the rack.

Glaze

¾ cup sifted confectioners' sugar
2 tbs. cream or milk
1 tsp. vanilla or kirsch

Thoroughly blend the glaze ingredients and spoon over the cooled cake. Serve the cake when the glaze hardens.

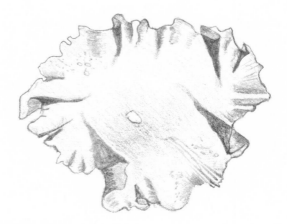

58. Laver *Porphyra perforata*

Laver is a somewhat elastic seaweed that looks like purple or reddish-brown cellophane. The individual pieces are 6 to 18 inches long. Look for it at low tide attached to other seaweeds or gather it on the beach after a storm. It is cultivated by the Japanese, who call it nori, and it can be eaten raw.

LAVER SEAWEED SOUP

1 cup fresh laver, or 2 oz. dried
3 cups soup stock (any stock will do, but one made
    with 4 cups water and 1½ tbs. miso paste is best;
    miso is found in most health food stores)
¼ cup peas
1 tbs. soy sauce
2 oz. egg noodles
4 scallions, finely chopped

Soak dried laver in warm water for 30 minutes. Cut into ¼-inch or smaller dice. Bring stock to boil, add laver and peas and simmer 20 minutes. Add soy sauce, noodles and any additional seasoning you like. Heat for 10 to 15 more minutes. Serve immediately with a sprinkling of chopped scallion on top of each bowl. Serves 4.

Variations: Substitute for noodles 2 cakes bean curd (tofu) cut into ½-inch cubes. Bean curd, made from soy beans, is available fresh in oriental food stores and canned in some gourmet or health-food shops. You may include any leftover meat or vegetables during the last 5 minutes of cooking. Ham, chicken, thinly sliced sausage, filet of sole or cod, tomatoes, carrots or spinach are but a few possibilities. Make this soup in the summer and substitute beach peas for the garden variety.

NITTY GRITTY SOURDOUGH

1½ cups sourdough starter
    (see January's recipe, page 22)
2 cups hot water
2½ cups unbleached white flour

Take the starter out of its container the night before you plan to make this bread and mix it with the 2 cups of water and 2½ cups of flour in a nonmetal bowl. Leave overnight in a warm place.

½ cup hominy grits
2½ cups boiling water
3 tbs. margarine
1 pkg. yeast dissolved in ½ cup warm water
2 tbs. salt
1 tsp. baking soda
¼ cup brown sugar or honey
8 to 9 cups unsifted unbleached white flour

The next morning put 1½ cups of the fermenting batter back into the starter container. Pour the grits into the 2½ cups boiling water and cook over low heat for 15 minutes, stirring occasionally. Melt small cubes of margarine into the grits, then pour the grits and margarine mixture into the batter. Let the batter cool to lukewarm and add the yeast. Combine the salt, brown sugar or honey, and soda, sprinkle over the batter and stir gently. Add enough flour to make a stiff bread dough, anywhere from 8 to 9 cups, and knead it on a floured counter or board until elastic, about 10 minutes. Put the dough in a greased bowl, grease the top and cover with a damp cloth. Put it in a warm place and let it rise until double, from 1 to 2 hours. Punch the dough down, divide it into thirds and place in 3 buttered loaf pans. Butter the tops of the loaves and cover them with a damp cloth. Let them rise in a warm place until double, from 1 to 2 hours. Bake in a 425° oven for 15 minutes then a 350° oven for 30 minutes, until the loaves make a hollow sound when tapped. Remove the loaves from their pans and let them cool on racks for 30 minutes before serving or freezing. Makes 3 loaves.

MUSSEL STUFFING

¼ cup mussels
¼ cup butter
1 stalk celery, finely chopped
1 small onion, finely chopped
1 clove garlic, minced
1½ to 2 cups lightly toasted bread cubes or stuffing mix
¾ cup mussel broth
    (add water if you don't have enough)
½ tsp. salt
3 grinds pepper
1 tbs. parsley, finely chopped
1 tsp. chervil, optional

Pick approximately 1 pt. of mussels, debeard, scrub and cook in 1 cup boiling water for 5 minutes or until the mussels are open. Remove the mussels from their shells and strain the broth through cheesecloth for later use.

Melt the butter and sauté the onion, celery and garlic for 5 minutes. Combine all the ingredients in a bowl and stuff the lightly salted cavity of a 3- to 5-lb. roasting bird. Double the recipe for a 6- to 9-lb. bird, triple it for a 10- to 12-lb. bird and quadruple it for a 13- to 15-lb. bird.

WILD NUT GRANOLA

1 18-oz. box old fashioned oatmeal
   (don't use the quick-cooked kind)
1¼ cups light or dark brown sugar
½ cup wheat germ (try honey-flavored
   wheat germ for variation)
½ cup shredded coconut
¼ tsp. salt
½ cup hickory nuts or black walnuts
   or a combination of both
½ cup peanut oil

Mix all the dry ingredients together. Add the oil; use your hands to mix everything thoroughly. Pour the granola into a 9 by 13 by 2-inch baking pan and bake in a 325° oven for 45 minutes. Every 15 minutes stir the mixture to prevent the bottom layer from sticking to the pan. Serve for breakfast with milk or yoghurt or sprinkle it on top of ice cream for dessert. Makes 20 servings.

RICE SALAD WITH SEA LETTUCE
AND GLASSWORT PICKLES

3 cups cooked white rice
½ cup chopped sea lettuce
2 tomatoes, chopped
1 cucumber, chopped
2 scallions, chopped
1 to 2 tsp. chopped glasswort pickles
⅓ cup homemade French dressing *(see page 19)*

Toss all the ingredients until they are well mixed. This salad is a great way to use up leftover rice. Serves 4.

December

$\mathcal{M}$ost of us can cope with December, feeling a basic pride in having successfully managed November. Nature can hardly be said to be cooperating; but at least we are not troubled by memories of a glorious October just passed. The year has made its final break with growth. The circle has closed. We are battening down for the winter passage. This gives us a sense of purpose and resolution.

Each day for the first three weeks of the month the arc made by the sun becomes smaller and smaller. It steadily rises farther and farther to the south and also sinks in an increasingly southerly quarter. Darkness expands its mastery and adds to its domain. The earth responds and we respond in turn, as man has for thousands of years. We respond physically with concerns for food, clothing and fuel. We respond on a magical or spiritual plane, having cleverly discovered a way to coax the sun to return, to insure the birth of life once again. December's celebrations, Christian, Jewish and pagan, all include in one way or another candlelight and joy and glowing colors.

Part of our Christmas lore concerns the far North and its quality of magic at this time of year. There is a special wild edible that seems to link the land of winter darkness, the home of the Christmas spirit and the people who live there: the lichen moss which grows on rocks. Lichen flourishes now (and whenever the temperature is not too hot and there is a reasonable amount of moisture). The reindeer of the North find the lichen delicate browsing; their Laplander masters also depend on it as a food source. Lichen custard may become a new addition to your Christmas menus. We serve our custard in delicate white *pots de crème* cups with gilt-edged covers to make this dessert more festive.

While you are in the woods gathering lichen from gray granite boulders, keep your eyes open for the bright Christmas colors of wintergreen. Our children make a game of finding the red berries they like to munch. Take the shiny green leaves home for tea to sip by the fire as you listen to music.

We dig our dandelion roots for blanched greens before the frost is really deep in the ground. Then we go to the sea with our children, who are first-class sea urchin pickers. These little hedgehogs of the shore usually grow in colonies. They are easy to gather at dead low tide and a pail fills up quickly, a welcome quality in December. But wear gloves to protect yourself from their spines. Get some periwinkles too while you are there.

It is beautiful to be in a warm kitchen in December. Fresh, dried or blanched wild edibles add new excitement to your traditional recipes. The fine smells of the year combine. The richness of all the seasons is yours.

BLACK WALNUT BUTTER

¼ cup finely chopped walnuts
¼ cup butter (kept at room temperature)
¼ tsp. sugar
¼ tsp. freshly ground nutmeg

Cream the walnuts, butter, sugar and nutmeg; taste, and add more sugar if desired. Spread the black walnut butter thinly on freshly toasted sourdough or French bread, and serve with wintergreen or birch tea. Serves 4 to 6.

BLACK WALNUT CAKE

1 cup butter or margarine
1 cup white sugar
1 cup brown sugar
5 eggs, separated

1 tsp. vanilla
3 cups flour
⅓ cup cornstarch
½ tsp. salt
2 cups black walnuts, chopped

Cream the butter or margarine until fluffy and gradually add the white and brown sugars. Beat the egg yolks until light and combine them with the butter, sugar and vanilla. Sift the flour, cornstarch and salt together into a 1-qt. bowl; beat the egg whites until stiff. Alternately fold in ¼ of the flour mixture and ¼ of the egg whites at a time into the batter. Combine all the mixtures and gently fold in the nuts. Butter and flour a tube or bundt pan and pour in the batter. Bake in a 350° oven for 1 hour and 15 minutes or until the cake tests done. Let the cake cool in its pan upside down on a rack for 1 hour before removing the pan. This cake cuts into much firmer and thinner pieces if you can possibly wait one day before serving it.

BLANCHED DANDELION GREENS

Early in December, before the ground freezes hard, dig up 20 or more dandelion plants and clip off the leaves to 1 inch from the roots. Place the plants in a tightly made wooden soda bottle or milk box or an old bureau drawer filled with sand. Place this box in a dark closet and water it every 3 days. Pale greenish-yellow leaves will grow in 2 to 3 weeks. Keep cutting and watering these greens and you should be able to harvest 2 to 3 crops of salad makings from your winter garden.

Blanched Dandelion Green Salad

4 cups blanched dandelion greens, washed and dried
1 scallion, finely chopped
¼ cup sliced radishes
1 clove garlic, minced
1 egg, hardboiled
4 tbs. olive oil
1½ tbs. wine vinegar
1 tbs. chopped parsley
½ tsp. salt
5 grinds pepper

Mash the egg yolk, garlic, and olive oil together in the bottom of a salad bowl until they form a smooth paste. Add the vinegar, parsley, salt and pepper, and toss the sliced egg white and radishes in the dressing. Add the blanched dandelion greens and toss until each leaf is coated with dressing. Serve immediately. Serves 4.

DRIED DAY LILY SOUP

¼ cup dried day lily blossoms
3 cups chicken stock, or 1 can chicken broth diluted with
    enough water to make 3 cups
¼ cup thinly sliced shreds of ham
1 tbs. soy sauce
1 tbs. white vinegar
1 tsp. salt
¼ tsp. black pepper
1 tbs. cornstarch dissolved in 2 tbs. water
1 egg
1 scallion, finely chopped

Put dried day lily blossoms in a nonmetal bowl, cover with 1 cup boiling water and allow to soak 30 minutes. If you forget to dry the day lilies in July and August, you can buy them in a Chinese grocery store as "golden needles." Bring the chicken broth to a boil, add the soaked day lilies, ham, soy sauce, vinegar, salt and pepper and simmer over medium heat for 4 minutes. Give the cornstarch mixture a quick stir and add it to the saucepan. Stir until the soup is slightly thickened. Beat the egg thoroughly and slowly pour it into the soup, stirring 4 times. Remove the soup from the heat and pour into soup bowls. Sprinkle the chopped scallion on top for garnish. Serves 4.

Variations: Add 4 shredded dried mushrooms, or ¼ cup shredded chicken, pork, or bamboo shoots for a heartier soup. Five drops of Chinese sesame seed oil on top of each serving add a unique flavor.

HONEY AND NUT ROLL

½ cup butter
2 cups flour
pinch of salt

1½ tbs. sugar
1½ tbs. sherry
1 egg yolk, beaten
1 tsp. lemon juice
3 to 6 tbs. honey
¾ cup chopped black walnuts, hickory or hazel nuts

Cut the butter into the flour with 2 knives or mash with a fork. Add salt, sugar, sherry, the beaten egg yolk and lemon juice to make a stiff paste. Add a little more flour if the dough is too sticky, or cold water if the dough is too stiff. Roll it into a rectangle approximately 9 by 13 inches. Brush a thin layer of honey on the surface and sprinkle with the chopped nuts. Roll up the pastry onto a baking sheet and cook in a 350° oven for 25 to 30 minutes. This is good for breakfast or dessert. Serves 6.

LICHEN CUSTARD

1 cup rock-tripe lichen
2 cups milk
1 cup cream
⅓ cup sugar
3 eggs, separated
1 tbs. sugar
1 tbs. rum or 1 tsp. vanilla

Bring 2 cups of water to a boil in the bottom section of a double boiler. Place the lichen and milk in the top section of the double boiler, set it over the boiling water and steam for 20 minutes over medium heat. Remove the pieces of lichen with a slotted spoon. Add the cream, ⅓ cup sugar and 3 egg yolks and beat with a whisk for 10 minutes or until the mixture thickens. Remove from heat and let the custard cool for 20 minutes. Meanwhile, beat the 3 egg whites until they begin to form peaks, add 1 tbs. sugar gradually and beat until soft peaks are formed. Fold the egg whites and rum into the cooled custard. You can eat it warm or cold after refrigerating it for 1 to 2 hours. This custard can also be used as a sauce over cake or fruit compote. Serves 4 to 6.

LICHEN RICE PUDDING

½ cup lichen, diced or crumbled into small pieces
⅓ cup raw rice

2 cups milk
⅓ cup sugar
⅛ tsp. freshly ground nutmeg
¼ tsp. almond extract
¼ cup chopped prunes
1 cup whipped cream

Bring 2 cups of water in the bottom section of a double boiler to a boil. Meanwhile place the lichen, rice and milk in the top section of a double boiler, cover, put it over the boiling water and steam it gently over low heat for 1½ hours. Remove the top double-boiler section from the heat and stir in the sugar, nutmeg, almond extract and prunes and let cool for 1 hour. Fold the whipped cream into the cooled pudding. You may want to reserve ¼ cup of the whipped cream to decorate the top of each serving later. Pour the pudding into 4 dessert bowls or parfait glasses and refrigerate for at least 1 hour. Serves 4.

DRIED MUSHROOM SOUP

⅓ cup dried mushrooms
1 cup boiling water
3 cups chicken broth
1 cup beef broth
2 tbs. butter
2 tbs. flour
¼ tsp. salt
4 grinds pepper
¼ cup sour cream

Place the dried mushrooms in a nonmetal bowl. Pour the boiling water over them and let stand for 30 minutes. Drain and chop the revived mushrooms. Place them in a saucepan with the chicken and beef broths and cook over medium heat until tender, approximately 10 to 20 minutes. Melt the butter in a small saucepan and add the flour, stirring constantly for 1 minute. Add ½ cup of the hot soup, stir until it thickens and pour the thickened mixture into the remaining soup. Continue stirring and add the salt, pepper and sour cream. Use a whisk, if necessary, to blend the sour cream. Taste, correct seasonings and serve immediately. Serves 4.

MUSSEL CURRY

2 qts. mussels
5 tbs. cooking oil
5 onions, diced
2 cloves garlic, minced
1 tsp. turmeric powder
2 tsp. coriander powder
1 tsp. prepared curry powder
¼ tsp. cayenne pepper (increase amount for hotter
    curry; or substitute chili powder)
½ tsp. ginger
1 16-oz. can tomatoes, cut up
1 small green pepper, diced
1½ cups mussel broth
1½ cups yoghurt
½ tsp. salt

Scrub, debeard and steam the mussels in 1 cup of water for 5 minutes. Remove the mussels from their shells and reserve. Strain the broth through cheesecloth if it seems sandy and reserve. Cook the onions and garlic in the oil over medium heat until they begin to brown. Add the seasonings (turmeric through ginger) and stir constantly for 3 more minutes. Add more oil if necessary to keep the onions and spices from sticking to the pan. Add the tomatoes and peppers and cook 10 minutes. Pour in the mussel broth, yoghurt and salt and cook over low heat 5 minutes. Taste and correct seasonings if necessary. Add the mussels and cook just long enough to heat them through, 2 to 5 minutes. Serves 4 to 6.

Variations: Use this curry sauce recipe for fish, meat or vegetable.

PERIWINKLES IN SNAIL SHELLS

72 periwinkles
24 snail shells (available in most gourmet shops)
¼ cup butter
8 cloves garlic, crushed in a garlic press
1 tbs. chopped parsley
¼ cup sourdough bread crumbs

Cook the periwinkles in 1 cup boiling water for 5 minutes. Let them cool and remove them from their shells with toothpicks or small skewers. Cream the butter and add the garlic, parsley and bread crumbs. Place three periwinkles in each snail shell and press about ½ tsp. of the herbed butter on top of the periwinkles. Bake the stuffed snail shells on a baking sheet in a 400° oven for 5 to 10 minutes or until the butter is melted. Serve immediately as an hors d'oeuvre. Serves 4.

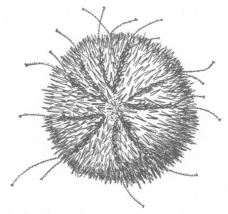

59. Sea Urchin

Strongylocentrotus drobachiensis

Look for sea urchins during low tide, in shallow water. They are sometimes found in tide pools, also. Green sea urchins are the most common, but they can be white, red-purple, brown or almost black. Carefully pry them off rocks when they are at least 2 to 4 inches in diameter.

SEA URCHIN APPETIZER

8 to 12 sea urchins at least 2 to 3 inches in diameter
2 lemons
sourdough or French bread

Sea urchins can be found in tide pools or just below the low tide line on rocky shores. We have found them clustered near beds of mussels. Remove them carefully. Their spines can prick so wear gloves. Rinse them in fresh water and cut each urchin in half with sharp scissors or a knife; place the sea urchin on a cutting board with its opening down (use a towel to hold it if the spines are sharp) and make the cut parallel to the plane of the board, or insert the pointed end of the scissors into the opening and enlarge it. Be careful to keep the spines out of the shell's interior. Remove and discard all the deep reddish-brown tissue with a demitasse spoon or a knife. Rinse the sea urchin under gently running water, leaving the light orange-yellow roe intact. Place the cleaned sea urchin halves on a small plate and squeeze some fresh lemon juice on top. Scoop out the roe with a spoon and take a bite. Try it on fresh sourdough or French bread, and discover a taste that is comparable to caviar. Serves 4 to 6.

WINTERGREEN (CHECKERBERRY) TEA

½ cup wintergreen leaves
1 qt. water
4 tsp. honey

Crush the leaves finely. (A Mouli Parsment parsley grater works well.) Bring the water to a boil and pour over the crushed leaves. Let the tea steep for at least 5 minutes and serve it with a teaspoon of honey in each cup. Serves 4.

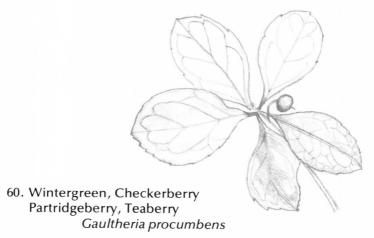

60. Wintergreen, Checkerberry
    Partridgeberry, Teaberry
        Gaultheria procumbens

Wintergreen is a low, creeping plant 2 to 6 inches high, growing in woods and open places. Pick the shiny, oval, dark evergreen leaves year round. These 1- to 2-inch-long leaves are very aromatic; crush one and smell its delicate wintergreen essence. White, waxy, bell-like blossoms are hidden under the leaves in July and August. Look for the bright-red wintergreen berries from October through March.

Guide to Easy Keeping

These foods keep so easily that they are worth noting. Refer to the particular month in this book (during which you gather each food), both introduction and drawing, for directions about collecting and drying or blanching.

Black Walnuts   Gather in October, see figure 57. Recipes for use in November and December.

Chicory Roots   Dig in late July (or August), see figure 38. Recipe for use in November.

Cranberry Sauce   Make according to October's recipe, see figure 54. Use in October and in November's Cranberry Cake.

Dandelion Roots   Dig in early December (or late November) for use in December and January, see figure 8. Recipe for use in December.

Day Lily Blossoms, Dried   Gather in July (or August), see figure 13. Recipe for use in December.

Hickory Nuts   Gather in October, see figure 55. Recipes for use in November and December.

Laver Seaweed, Dried   Gather year round, see figure 58. Recipe for use in November.

Mushrooms, Dried   Gather in May, July, August and September (and early October), see figures 22, 33, 40, 42, 45, and 51. Recipe for use in December.

Red and White Clover Blossoms, Dried   Gather in May (through September), see figure 21. Recipe for use in November.

Sea Lettuce   Gather year round, see figure 6. Recipes for use in February and July.

Books of Related Interest

Amos, William H. *The Life of the Seashore.* New York: McGraw Hill, 1966.

Christensen, Clyde M. *Common Edible Mushrooms.* Minneapolis: University of Minnesota Press, 1943.

Fernald, Merritt Lyndon, Alfred Charles Kinsey, and Reed C. Rollins. *Edible Wild Plants of North America.* New York: Harper and Row, 1958.

Gibbons, Euell. *Stalking the Blue-Eyed Scallop.* New York: David McKay Co., 1964.

————. *Stalking The Healthful Herbs.* New York: David McKay Co., 1966.

————. *Stalking The Wild Asparagus.* New York: David McKay Co., 1962.

Grimm, William Carey. *The Book of Shrubs.* Harrisburg: Stackpole Books, 1957.

Hertzberg, Ruth and Beatrice Vaughan. *Putting Food by.* Brattleboro, Vermont: Stephen Greene, 1972.

Kieran, John. *An Introduction to Nature.* Garden City, N.J.: Doubleday & Company, Inc., 1966.

Medsger, Oliver Perry. *Edible Wild Plants.* New York: Macmillan, 1939.

Miller, Orson K., Jr. *Mushrooms of North America.* New York: E. P. Dutton and Co., 1972.

Peterson, Roger Tory and Margaret McKenny. *A Field Guide to Wildflowers.* Boston: Houghton Mifflin, 1968.

Petrides, George A. *A Field Guide to Trees and Shrubs (Northeastern and Central North America).* Boston: Houghton Mifflin, 1958.

Smith, Alexander H. *The Mushroom Hunter's Field Guide Revised and Enlarged.* Ann Arbor: University of Michigan Press, 1963.

Thomas, William Sturgis. *Field Book of Common Mushrooms.* New York and London: G. P. Putnam, 1948.

Index